The Unexplained:

Paranormal Encounters in the UK

A guide to the strange tales of cryptids, ghost stories and UFO sightings from around the UK

Contents

Foreword	11
Introduction	15

Cryptozoology 23

The Beast Of Bodmin Moor	27
The Benbecula Mermaid	32
The Knucker of Lyminster	37
The Loch Ness Monster	42
Dobar-Chu	49
Winged Snakes	55
The Black Dog of Bungay	61
Black-Eyed Children	66
The Pigman	73
The Owlman	79
The Beast of Brassknocker Hill	83
The Stronsay Beast	88
Honourable mentions	92

Hauntings, Ghosts & Spirits 97

Pluckley Village - Kent	102
Enfield Poltergeist - London	112
Blickling Hall - Norwich	119
Pendle Hill - Lancashire	127
Borley Rectory - Essex	136
Ancient Ram Inn - Gloucestershire	142
Chillingham Castle - Northumberland	149
Berry Pomeroy Castle - Devon	156

Samlesbury Hall - Lancashire	162
Buckland Abbey - Devon	169
Felbrigg Hall - Norfolk	173
St Briavels Castle - Wye Valley	178
Whitby Abbey - Whitby, Yorkshire	183
Tower of London - London	189
Aston Hall - Birmingham	193
Station Hotel - Dudley	196
Eyam - Derbyshire	202
The Red Lion Inn - Avebury	206
Stirling Castle - Scotland	211
Honourable mentions	216

UFOs & Alien Sightings 223

The Warminster 'Thing'	230
The Calvine UFO photo	237
The Rendlesham Forest Incident	241
The Sheffield Triangles	246
Broad Haven School	251
Berwyn Mountain Incident	255
Robert Taylor/Dechmont woods Incident	260
Clapham Wood	263
Bonnybridge Sightings - Falkirk Triangle	267
West Freugh Incident	271
Lakenheath - Bentwaters	277
Exercise Mainbrace	282
Honourable mentions	287

Closing Thoughts & Theories 291

References 303

This book is dedicated to my wife, Luna and all of our children, Morgan, Jack, Noah, Charlie and Harper-Rose. Without them, and their love and patience, this book would not be possible.

Acknowledgements

I would like to take this opportunity to thank my good friend, Alan Hackett, for kick-starting my interest in the UFO subject all those years ago, which in turn reignited my love for all things paranormal. Without you, this book would never have happened.

I'd also like to say a more general word of thanks to all of my friends, with whom I have spent countless hours discussing these cases and more, usually well into the early hours of the morning. Thank you for listening to me, and putting up with my rambling.

DISCLAIMER

Every effort has been made to ensure that all copyright holders of any material included in this book have been traced. However, if any copyright holder has been inadvertently overlooked, we apologise and request that they contact the publisher so that any necessary corrections can be made.

The information presented in this book is believed to be accurate and reliable at the time of publication. However, given the broad scope of topics covered and the possibility of changes occurring over time, such as dates or other specific information, some inaccuracies may be present. If you notice any errors, please contact the publisher or author with evidence, and we will make the necessary revisions.

This book does not have the endorsement of, nor does it endorse, any of the businesses or establishments that provide ghost tours or opportunities for paranormal investigations.

The publisher and author disclaim any legal liability or responsibility for any errors or omissions that may have occurred in the production of this book.

Foreword

The world is a vast and fascinating place. From the complex mathematics that exists behind nature. From the huge variety of flora and fauna, to the very meaning of human consciousness, the planet we live on is a source of constant wonder. And alongside this exists the world's mainstream science, dictating to us what to believe. Most of us are taught this from an early age at school. We are told the way the world works by others who are qualified to do so.

But for some people, this is not enough. We start to question whether the world really is as we've been told. Whether science really does have all the answers. It is of course completely logical to do so. Science is in a continual state of flux. As new discoveries are made, and tests are performed to validate these discoveries, ideas are superseded and revised.

This leads some to start looking into the mysterious world of the paranormal. Be it ghostly phenomena, sightings of strange beasts or experiences with non-human craft and beings, there's a lot going on out there which, according to mainstream science, should not exist!

For most, just looking into these cases and allowing it to shape their view of the world is enough. But some people feel the urge to delve deeper. To start to investigate cases, speak directly with witnesses and release this information to the wider public. Sometimes these individuals may decide to investigate the world of the paranormal on a general level. Other times they may choose to focus on particular areas of interest.

This is something I experience on a day-to-day basis. Since early 2008 I have actively investigated UFO sightings and alien encounters for Birmingham UFO Group. In 2009 I also took on chairman responsibilities for the group, and have been running it ever since. One of the aspects of B.U.F.O.G. that I am most proud of is our monthly meetings. Ever since its inception, the group has always had an active community of attendees.

It is through this community that I first met Nathan Lockley. It soon became apparent to me that he had a genuine fascination with the world of the paranormal, and that we also shared a number of other interests. It was only natural that we should become good friends! I know full well the amount of effort and dedication it takes to be an active investigator, and I can definitely vouch for Nathan in this regard. For many years he has recorded and released podcasts via Paraverse, has published reports on cases he has looked into and he has built an active community on social media through U.P.R.I.S.I.N.G. UFO and Paranormal Investigation group. And now he has released this book.

If, like me, you live in the United Kingdom, you'll no doubt be astounded by the many bizarre and intriguing incidents which have taken place close to home. But this book is not just for Brits! If you happen to live elsewhere, you'll still be amazed by the incredible number of unusual events that have taken place on our rather modestly sized-island. So relax, perhaps grab yourself a hot drink, and prepare yourself for a fascinating journey!

Dave Hodrien
Birmingham UFO Group Chairman & Lead Investigator
United Kingdom Deputy Representative for ICER (the International Coalition for Extraterrestrial Research)

Introduction

Have you ever seen a ghost or heard footsteps or voices when there is nobody there? Ever seen lights in the sky moving in strange ways you can't explain? Are you intrigued by stories of peculiar creatures seen wandering around woodland or mountains? Unsure whether you are correct to believe in any of this or if you are just going crazy? Maybe you are just interested in the paranormal, particularly the paranormal history of the UK and are looking for some interesting places and cases to get started on. Then you are in the right place.

This is a collection of paranormal, strange, unusual, and sometimes even downright crazy sightings from around the United Kingdom. From the Loch Ness monster, to 'Britain's Roswell', we will look at the strangest things claimed to have been witnessed. We will look into each sighting, delving into what is believed to have been seen, and then looking for other possible explanations. Firstly, we need to understand, what IS paranormal? What does it mean? And what type of thing does this term cover?

The word paranormal is a broad term, but it generally means "denoting events or phenomena that are beyond the scope of normal scientific understanding." Examples of this would be things such as telekinesis, psychics, ghosts or spirits, cryptozoology, and UFOs. The scientific community regards these topics as nonsense and class them all as 'pseudoscience'. Pseudoscience is "a belief or practice, such as believing in ghosts or trying to make contact with them, that is mistakenly regarded as being based on the scientific method".

So it is safe to say the scientific community, in general, does not approve of this subject, and does not spend any time or money investigating 'evidence' found by amateur investigators, regardless of how compelling it may be. If you asked a paranormal investigator, they would most likely tell you this is down to the fact that these experiences can not be measured scientifically, and that they use forces and energies not currently accepted or understood by science.

Just as science and the scientific method go back thousands of years, so do tales of the paranormal. Even as far back as the first century A.D. when the Roman author, Pliny the Younger, wrote one of the earliest ghost stories in a letter. He reported the spirit of a bearded old man, rattling chains in his home in Athens. There are countless stories of spirits of the dead coming back to visit loved ones throughout history, with many seeing this as proof of life after death.

There are various types of paranormal experiences, and there are even more explanations and opinions for what these could be. Some are logical, some much more unusual. With UFOs, some believe we are being visited by extraterrestrial life, or possibly life from another dimension and some believe all of these sightings can be easily explained by mundane, natural things such as misidentified aircraft or weather phenomena. People who claim to see apparitions or ghosts, believe them to be the spirits or the souls of the dead. Whereas sceptics would put these sightings down to things such as pareidolia (the tendency of the human mind to see meaningful things like faces in patterns or ambiguous visual stimuli) or misinterpreting things such as shadows caused by an outside influence that may not have been noticed by an investigator or witness.

As the paranormal subject is more than a little on the strange side of science, investigators and people trying to understand these phenomena have found some strange ways to try to measure, record or interpret this evidence over the years. As technology has gotten better, it is being used more and more in investigations, especially in the search for spirits. You only have to search for 'ghost hunters' on platforms like Youtube and you will be inundated by people claiming to have found proof of these phenomena. You will also notice a lot of technology being used. The type of technology these investigators use include:

- EMF (electromagnetic field) detectors: These are used as it is believed that ghosts and spirits need 'energy' to manifest and they either use the EMF around us to do this or they give off their electromagnetic field as they do this. Fluctuations detected on EMF detectors are claimed to be proof of this manifesting happening nearby.
- Electronic thermometers: Sudden hot or cold spots are also believed to be signs

that spirits are using the energy in the air around us to manifest. Digital thermometers can be used to point at an exact spot to test for temperature changes.
- Voice recorders: These are used to capture EVP (electronic voice phenomena) or quiet voices or whispers that were not heard by people present at an investigation. They are also useful for capturing evidence that can be recorded and reviewed after an investigation.
- Ouija boards: The belief behind these boards is that they can be used to directly communicate with any spirits present at the time of the investigation and that the energy needed for ghosts to communicate this way is much lower than that needed for temperature changes, EVP and EMF, so a much more detailed message can be received this way.
- Spirit boxes: These are like radios that scan through all radio waves listening for words that come through as answers to questions or messages for people present.
- Cameras: This one seems kind of self-explanatory, but cameras can be used to

film and record an investigation for a more thorough search for visual and sound evidence later on. They can also be used to photograph a space, as many believe that cameras can capture spirits that cannot be seen by the naked eye.
- Many other apps on smartphones: Some claim to detect movement using the camera whereas others claim to use their own EMF detector to power a soundboard with a limited dictionary for spirits to communicate.

Before all of this technology was available, there were other ways used to attempt to communicate with spirits. This included using bells for sound, asking for the spirits to knock or bang on walls, and dowsing rods used to pick up energy or even to answer questions. Most people also believed the best piece of equipment we all have is our own bodies. Our own five senses are said to be the most sensitive and trustworthy. There are still many investigators who prefer to use the 'old ways' as they believe they get better evidence and that the more technical equipment can be easily influenced by other things such as bad wiring or smartphones giving off their own electromagnetic fields.

Investigations into other types of paranormal subjects, like UFOs and cryptozoology, would use a lot less technology. Cameras and smartphone cameras are the most widely used equipment to capture evidence of these phenomena. These two subjects may still be classed as paranormal, but the scientific community seems a *little* more open-minded where they are concerned, but usually on a case-by-case basis.

Big cat sightings, for example, will be investigated and believed with good enough evidence, a lot more than claims of something like vampires would be. And UFOs have become less of a taboo subject in just the last few years after the US government has openly admitted that they have had sightings and cannot explain what they are. At the time of writing, these sightings are now being investigated by NASA scientists, as well as the US government themselves.

But back in the UK, there have been stories of some strange and unusual sightings all over the British isles and throughout history. For such a small area, there are hundreds of tales of giants, fairies, werewolves and even our very own bigfoot. It seems if you travel to any area of the UK, you can find locals who will tell you the legend of the nearest 'beast' or 'creature'.

So what better place to start than there, with Cryptozoology.

CRYPTOZOOLOGY

Cryptozoology, the study of unknown or undiscovered animals, has fascinated people around the world for centuries. From tales of sea serpents to sightings of Bigfoot, cryptids have captivated the imaginations of both scientists and enthusiasts alike.

The history of cryptozoology can be traced back to ancient civilizations, with tales of mythical beasts and legendary creatures. However, it wasn't until the late 19th and early 20th centuries that cryptozoology began to be recognized as a legitimate scientific pursuit.

One of the most famous examples of a cryptid is the Loch Ness Monster, a legendary creature said to inhabit the depths of Loch Ness in Scotland. Sightings of the creature have been reported for centuries, but it wasn't until 1933 that the modern era of Loch Ness Monster sightings began. Since then, numerous expeditions and investigations have been conducted in an attempt to prove the creature's existence.

Another well-known cryptid is Bigfoot, also known as Sasquatch, a tall, ape-like creature said to roam the forests of North America. Sightings of Bigfoot have been reported for decades, and hundreds, if not thousands, of people have dedicated their lives to searching for proof of its existence.

Other notable cryptids include the Chupacabra, a creature said to attack and drink the blood of livestock in Latin America, and the Mothman, a winged creature said to haunt the town of Point Pleasant, West Virginia.

While sceptics may dismiss the existence of these creatures, cryptozoologists continue to search for evidence that may one day prove their existence. So let's get stuck into what are, in my humble opinion, some of the best and most famous cryptid cases the UK has to offer, examining the 'evidence' that supports their existence. Whether you're a believer or a sceptic, the world of cryptozoology is sure to intrigue anyone.

The Beast Of Bodmin Moor

Bodmin Moor

The Beast Of Bodmin story is probably the UK's best-known big-cat legend. First sighted in 1983, the creature has been described as a 'phantom wild cat' with two prominent sharp teeth, most likely a leopard, and has been regularly reported to the police ever since.

Bodmin Moor itself is 208 square kilometres (80 sq miles) in size. It includes Cornwall's highest point, Brown Willy, which is a hill 1,378 feet (420 metres) above sea level. Bodmin Moor is also the source of many of Cornwall's rivers, such as the River Fowey and the River Tiddy. It is also home to the Jamaica Inn, a traditional Inn built in 1750, that is also said to be haunted.

One of the reports of this cryptid was from a worried member of the public who claimed the 'beast' was at the top of his garden, "digesting his dinner". In October 2016, near St Austell, a man named John Parkinson photographed what he believed to be the footprints of the beast. He held a tape measure against the prints and showed they were 4 inches wide.

This led to many locals believing a big cat was definitely in the area, and they obviously became worried. Nearby, a few months prior, there was another sighting by a driver known as Duncan, who claimed a creature leapt out in front of him. He called the police who came out to investigate and found more prints and also a decapitated deer nearby. There have been reports of other mutilated or half-eaten animals in the area since the first sighting of Bodmin's beast. One poor gentleman even found a severed dog leg in his garden, supposedly left there by a big cat.

Another witness, 72-year-old retired salesman Sid Yates, claims to have spotted the creature one morning in July 2013. When asked about his experience the next day, he said "I came out of my house yesterday morning at 9 am, and as I looked up the lane about 50 yards, in front of me was the Beast of Bodmin." He went on to describe the creature as looking "a bit like a black labrador but it had long legs, a tail and a flat nose." He was determined it was the Beast and not a dog he saw before him that morning, as many sceptics claimed. He also claims that this was his third sighting of the big black cat.

So how did these 'cats' get here? Well, one of the most popular theories is, along with most 'wild big cat' stories, that these animals had been illegally kept as pets and then set free into the wild, either accidentally escaping or released on purpose to avoid being arrested or fined if found with them in their homes.

Another theory was that after Plymouth Zoo was forced to close down in 1978, three Pumas were being moved to Dartmoor Zoo. However, they never arrived. They were supposedly set free by Plymouth zoo owner Mary Chipperfield who, rather than see them placed into another zoo, decided to let her favourite breeding pair, and another young male, go free into the wild. This theory was confirmed nearly forty years later by Benjamin Mee, the Dartmoor zoo owner since 2006. He wasn't sure exactly how they got out, but he confirmed that there should have been three Pumas at Dartmoor Zoo that were not there and that they were coming from Plymouth Zoo.

Danny Bamping, founder of the British Big Cat Society said that at the time that the cats could have easily survived on the moor, and even strayed into other areas with big cat sightings. He also said that Mary Chipperfield claimed to have broken down white transporting five cats, and somehow three of them escaped. Mary passed away in 2014, but her husband denies any claims that she released any animals into the wild.

This may seem like an acceptable theory for how these wild cats got into the area, but how have three cats supposedly survived for over forty years? The average lifespan of a Puma is between 8-13 years. Assuming they lived to their oldest possible age, and if they were breeding and their cubs lived for this long too, could this explain the sightings in Bodmin?

The Ministry of Agriculture, Fisheries and Food investigated the sightings in 1995 and found that there was "no verifiable evidence" of exotic cats in the wild in Britain. Less than a week after the investigation, a large cat skull was found. Measuring about 4 inches (10 cm) long

30

by 7 inches (18 cm) wide, the skull was lacking its lower jaw but possessed three sharp, prominent canines that suggested that it might have been a leopard.

The story hit the national press at about the same time as the official denial of alien big cat evidence on Bodmin Moor. The skull was sent to the National History Museum in London for analysis. They found that the skull was genuinely from a young male leopard, but that it had not been killed in Britain, and was imported as part of a leopard skin rug.

So what could this creature be? Is it truly a leopard or a black panther roaming the moors? Is it just a normal-sized feline photographed to make it look bigger against the background? Are the footprints just those of a big dog being walked in the area? If so, what about the animal mutilations and the witness testimonies of those claiming to have seen the creature up close? Maybe one day in the future, we will finally get answers to these questions.

The Benbecula Mermaid

The Benbecula Coast

Tales of mermaids could very well be the oldest of the stories of strange creatures that we do not understand. Seen all over the world and throughout history, I could probably write a whole book on mermaid sightings alone. In fact, many have done just this.

Most sightings have been explained away as whale or dolphin sightings, even manatees or sightings of actual people swimming in the sea. But some accounts have become as legendary as the mermaids themselves.

C.J.S. Thompson, a former curator at the Royal College of Surgeons of England, notes in his book - The Mystery and Lore of Monsters, that "Traditions concerning creatures half-human and half-fish in form have existed for thousands of years, and the Babylonian deity Era or Oannes, the Fish-god is usually depicted as having a bearded head with a crown and a body like a man, but from the waist downwards he has the shape of a fish." Greek mythology contains stories of the god Triton, the merman messenger of the sea, and several modern religions including Hinduism and Candomble (an Afro-Brazilian belief) worship mermaid goddesses to this day.

Most young children would associate mermaids with Disney's "the little mermaid" but if that film had used the descriptions from witnesses, that particular classic animated film would be classed as a horror movie, with the terrifying mermaids in the 2011 film "Pirates of the Caribbean: On Stranger Tides" a closer match to the legendary creatures.

Although that doesn't mean all tales of mermaids are bad. There are stories of them befriending and even marrying men from land, even growing legs and becoming human once they have found love. But most stories, especially the more recent and less mythical sightings, are usually just that; sightings. With a lot less interaction with the creatures, if any at all. And it is one such sighting that we are going to explore.

1830, at Sgeir na Duchadh, near Grimnis on the west coast of the Outer Hebridean island of Benbecula, a group of people were harvesting seaweed. One of the women went to wash her feet at the end of the reef and while she was doing so, she heard a splashing sound. When she looked in the direction of the sound, she spotted a creature a few feet away in the water. She looked like a "woman in miniature". This miniature woman started to do somersaults and was splashing around. Startled, the witness called for the others working nearby to come and see the creature. They all stood and watched in amazement for a while until some of the men went into the water to try to capture the 'woman', but she evaded their efforts. While she was swimming away, a boy aimed and threw a rock at the mermaid and struck her on the back. She cried out in pain and disappeared down into the water. The locals all stood in amazement and shock, unable to believe what they had just seen with their own eyes.

A few days later, a strange creature washed up on a nearby beach at Culle Bay near Nunton, which is just a few miles north of the original sighting. The creature was described as having the upper body shape of a well-developed woman but was around the size of a 4-year-old girl but with abnormally developed breasts. She had long dark glossy hair and her skin was white, soft and tender. However, her lower half was described as being "like a salmon but without the scales". Large crowds began to gather and those present concluded that this was, in fact, the body of a mermaid.

The local sheriff was called and upon seeing the body, he called for a shroud and coffin to be brought to the beach. The story goes on to say that the mermaid's body was then laid into this coffin and buried in the nearby churchyard. It was also said that the funeral for this creature was one of the largest attended on the island and that, as the creature appeared to be human, was carried out like any other Christian burial. There have been some contradicting theories on the resting place of the mermaid, as there is no grave marker relating to this creature in the nearby churchyard. Other theories suggest that she was buried on the beach near the dunes, close to where she washed up. A recent survey was carried out on a large stone near the south end of the bay, suspecting that this may have been her final resting place but it was inconclusive.

So what do you think? Are mermaids real? And if so, did the locals of Benbecula witness one with their own eyes? Or is this just a case of a story being told and retold over the years and becoming more fantastical and just another one of the legendary tales of the unexplainable in the UK?

Perhaps another study of the beach where the body was supposedly laid to rest will find some evidence that there was in fact a mermaid buried there. Perhaps the body itself will one day be found, proving once and for all that there really are creatures out there that science just refuses to believe in.

The most likely scenario is that this will remain unproven one way or the other and will forever be a tale told and passed down through generations of locals and retold to tourists, hoping to catch a glimpse of the elusive mermaids in Benbecula.

The Knucker of Lyminster

The Church at Lyminster

This could be one of the most famous British stories, you didn't even know you had heard of. There are countless tales of knights slaying dragons throughout history. They have inspired books and poems and have been portrayed in tv shows, films and children's cartoons. Where most stories of this type are impossible to substantiate, there are a few that may be traceable. The Knucker of Lyminster, along with a few other stories of Knuckers around Sussex, may very well have been the inspiration for many if not most of these tales. The name "Knucker", sometimes also known as

"Nucker", comes from the Anglo-Saxon word Nicor which means "water monster" or "water dragon". The Knucker was said to have wings and was described as a 'sea serpent' with a long tail and four legs.

The name was given to the creatures supposedly living in "Knucker holes". Knucker holes are small pools of water that are said to be bottomless. One such pool was located not far from the church in the village of Lyminster, West Sussex.

Legend has it that during the middle ages, Sussex had a dragon problem. The Knuckers that lived in these pools of water would consume livestock and even villagers that wandered too close to their Knucker hole. The people in the villages surrounding these holes grew angry with the loss of animals and villagers and so they complained to the king of Sussex. He sent out knights to slay these dragons and rid these pools of the creatures living within them. All but one were slain by the king's knights, but none were able to slay the beast living in Lyminster. So the king offered his daughter's hand in marriage to whoever killed the creature. The offer was taken up by a knight-errant, a knight wandering the kingdom in search of adventures hoping to prove his chivalric values.

Once the dragon was dead, he married the king's daughter and they both stayed in Lyminster and lived there until their deaths. The stone, claimed to be from the grave of the knight, was said to stand in the graveyard at the church at Lyminster until recently when it was taken inside the church to be kept safe from weathering. The mediaeval stone, known as the slayer's slab, stands inside the church to this day. The stone itself has no name or markings to suggest to whom it belonged.

As with other stories of this nature, there are contradicting theories depending on who you speak to. Some locals in Lyminster would tell this tale differently. They tell of a local farmer's boy by the name of Jim Pulk (or Jim Puttock) who outwitted the dragon. The Mayor of Arundel offered a reward for the killing of the Knucker and so the boy cooked and poisoned a giant pie, took it to the Knucker hole by horse and cart and used them as bait. The Knucker ate the horse, cart and pie and was killed by the poison. The boy then took the head of the monster to the local pub to celebrate but dropped dead moments later. It is believed that he wiped his mouth but had forgotten to wash the poison from his hands. In this story, the slayer's slab belonged to this Farmer's boy.

There are also numerous stories surrounding the 'Knucker holes' themselves. Recent tests have shown the pool at Lyminster to be around 30 feet deep, however, local legend states that villagers tied 6 bellropes from the church tower together and lowered them into the pool and still didn't reach the bottom. It is believed that a strong underwater spring fed the pool and this may have led the locals to believe it was bottomless.

As well as the slayer's slab, there are a few other things you may find in and around Lyminster that appear to be inspired by this story. The local pub is named The Six Bells after the ropes used to measure the depth of the pool, and there is a stained glass window inside St Mary Magdalene's church that depicts the Knucker being fed a pie by the local farmer's boy.

So was a mediaeval species of giant reptile feeding on the livestock and occupants of a small Sussex village in the middle ages? Was said creature then killed? If so, who do you believe killed it? The brave knight who claimed the king's daughter as his wife? Or was it the local boy who outwitted the beast, only to be killed by the same poison?

The tale of the Knucker of Lyminster is perhaps the best example of a story steeped in folklore, with legends of kings, knights slaying dragons and mediaeval gravestones. There may or may not have also been a poisoned pie involved.

The Loch Ness Monster

Loch Ness

The Loch Ness Monster, also known as "Nessie," is one of the most enduring and iconic legends in the world of cryptozoology. For centuries, people have reported seeing a large, elusive creature in the dark, murky waters of Loch Ness, a deep freshwater lake located in the Scottish Highlands. Despite extensive scientific studies and countless eyewitness accounts, the true nature of the Loch Ness Monster remains shrouded in mystery.

The first recorded sighting of Nessie dates back to the 6th century when a man named Saint

Columba reportedly encountered a creature while crossing the lake. According to legend, the creature had just killed a man who was swimming in the lake and was approaching Saint Columba with menacing intent. Saint Columba is said to have made the sign of the cross and commanded the creature to leave, at which point it promptly disappeared beneath the surface of the water.

Over the centuries, reports of sightings of the Loch Ness Monster continued to surface, with many locals and visitors to the area claiming to have seen a large, serpentine creature swimming in the lake. However, it was not until the 20th century that the Loch Ness Monster became a global phenomenon.

In 1933, a newspaper reported the first modern sighting of the Loch Ness Monster. George Spicer, a London-based businessman, claimed to have seen a "most extraordinary form of animal" while driving near the lake with his wife. According to Spicer, the creature was about 25 feet long and had a long, narrow neck, which it held out of the water. The sighting sparked a media frenzy, and soon other reports of sightings began to flood in.

One of the most famous and widely-cited sightings of the Loch Ness Monster occurred in 1934 when a surgeon named Robert Kenneth Wilson claimed to have captured the first-ever photograph of the cryptid. The photograph, which shows a dark, blurry shape in the water, became known as the "surgeon's photograph" and is still widely debated among cryptozoologists and sceptics today.

In the years that followed, there were numerous other sightings of the Loch Ness Monster, each adding new details to the creature's legend. Many witnesses reported seeing a long, serpentine neck and humps that appeared and disappeared beneath the water's surface. Others claimed to have seen the creature swimming at high speeds, diving deep beneath the water, or even leaping out of the water like a whale.

Despite the abundance of sightings and eyewitness accounts, scientists have been unable to provide any concrete evidence of the Loch Ness Monster's existence. Numerous scientific studies have been conducted over the years, including extensive sonar scans and underwater searches of the lake, but none have been able to definitively prove the creature's existence.

Some sceptics believe that the sightings of the Loch Ness Monster are simply the result of hoaxes, misidentifications of known animals, or the power of suggestion. Others point out that the lake is so large and so deep that it is entirely possible for an elusive creature to remain hidden in its depths.

One of the most famous and controversial pieces of evidence in the search for the Loch Ness Monster is the so-called "Dinsdale film." In 1960, a man named Tim Dinsdale captured footage of a large, dark shape moving through the water. The footage shows a long, serpentine neck and a head with a distinctly horse-like shape, leading many cryptozoologists to believe that Dinsdale had captured footage of the elusive creature. However, sceptics argue that the footage could also easily be explained as a hoax or a misidentification of known animals.

So what do people actually think is being seen out in the deep dark waters of this famous Scottish loch? Many believers in Nessie believe the creature to be a plesiosaur, or another such large animal, that has survived in the loch for the last 65 million years since they were thought to have become extinct. They would claim that the loch is big enough and deep enough to keep such an animal alive. Sceptics argue against this, claiming that the loch would not be big enough for the large population of these creatures that would be needed for them to have been able to successfully breed and stay alive for so long in a lake.

In June 2018, a scientific study of the loch took and studied DNA samples from the water, taking more than 250 water samples from the surface and depths of the lake over a two-week period. They then amplified tiny amounts of genetic material DNA in the samples to detect different plant and animal species, from cells they had left in the waters of the loch or in the water that had run off from the land nearby. There were no traces of 'monster' DNA, no plesiosaurs. But they did find something intriguing that they believed could explain the serpentine creature described by witnesses.

The results of the environmental DNA survey conducted by Neil Gemmell, a geneticist from Otago University in New Zealand, indicate that there is no evidence of the presence of giant reptiles or aquatic dinosaurs in the lake.

According to Gemmell, the survey uncovered traces of DNA from over 3,000 species, such as fish, deer, pigs, birds, humans, and bacteria, living in or near Loch Ness. But "we did not find any giant reptiles; we didn't find any reptiles at all". "We tested a variety of ideas about giant sturgeons or catfish that might be here from time to time, but we did not find those either."

One thing the researchers *did* find is that Loch Ness contains a lot of eels. And the researchers say it is possible, although unlikely, that sightings of Nessie may actually be sightings of overgrown eels. "Out of the 250-odd water samples we took, pretty much every sample has got eels in it," claims Gemmell. "But are they giant eels? I don't know."

So how big can eels get? Could this really be what people have been seeing for all of these years? There are two known eel species in the UK, the European eel and the Conger eel. European eels are usually around 2-2.6 ft, and rarely get bigger than 3ft 3in, but have been known to grow to around 4ft 11in, in exceptional circumstances. The conger eel is usually a little larger but is usually only found in the ocean. They have been known to grow up to 6ft in length.

So as you can imagine, an eel moving along the surface of the water may give the "serpentine" appearance of this mythical creature, but they definitely don't explain the size descriptions of Nessie by witnesses.

So, is Loch Ness home to an ancient plesiosaur, left over from the time of the dinosaurs? Is it some kind of freakishly large eel? Is it something entirely different? Or is the whole thing a hoax, with people adding their 'sightings' to become part of the legend? I personally think this legend is so big now, that even with undeniable scientific proof that the Nessie isn't real, nothing would stop some from believing the tales and probably won't stop future sightings from occurring.

Dobar-Chu

Lough Mask in County Mayo

Most of the stories of this strange creature are not actually found in the UK, but as you will see, it may have links to others that are. The Dobhar-Chu (pronounced doo-war-coo) is a fabled creature that is said to inhabit the waters of Ireland, particularly in the area around Lough Mask in County Mayo. The creature, whose name roughly translated, means 'water hound' or 'hound of the deep', is often described as a large, otter-like animal with a dog-like head and a long, serpentine tail. It is thought to be around 7ft long, and around the size of a crocodile. In fact, it is also known as the Irish crocodile.

The Dobhar-Chu, a savage and gruesome creature, is said to inhabit the depths of lakes, rivers, and even the sea, and is believed to be capable of traversing vast distances both in water and on land. This ferocious beast is infamous for its remarkable speed, aggressiveness, and voracious appetite for human flesh. According to legend, there are typically two of these monsters, and if one of them is slain, its mate will emerge from the watery depths to seek revenge on the assailant, often by hunting them down and devouring them. This phenomenon is thought to occur because the Dobhar Chu emits a spine-chilling, high-pitched whistle as it nears death, which serves as a warning to its mate.

The legend of the Dobhar-Chu has been passed down through generations, and there have been several reported sightings of the creature over the years.

The first recorded sighting of the Dobhar-Chu was reported in 1684 when a man named John McAdam was said to have been attacked and killed by the creature while fishing on Lough

Mask. According to legend, McAdam had ventured out onto the lake in his boat when he suddenly saw the creature swimming towards him. He attempted to row back to shore, but the Dobhar-Chu caught up to him and dragged him under the water. McAdam's body was later found on the shore, with the creature still clinging to him.

There have been several other reported sightings of the Dobhar-Chu. In 1722, a woman named Grace McGloighlin (also known as Grace Connolly) was washing clothes on the shore of Glenade Lough. Reports state that her husband, Terrence, rushed down to the edge of the lough when he heard his wife's screams, but he was too late. He found his wife's mutilated body, with the Dobhar-Chu sleeping on top of it. He ran home to get a dagger and returned to kill the beast. As the creature died, it let out a scream which seemed to summon its mate. The second Dobhar-Chu then attacked Terrence, and after a long and bloodied battle, the second beast was killed. Another very interesting part of this story is that a gravestone with the name Grace Connolly, and with mention of a husband named Terrence, actually exists in the cemetery at Drummans, which is part of the approach to the Valley of Glenade. It also depicts her killer... with a carved image of the Dobhar-Chu.

Another famous sighting of the creature occurred in 1948 when a man named Tom McClelland was said to have encountered the creature while fishing on Lough Glenade in County Leitrim. McClelland reported seeing a large, otter-like animal with a dog-like head swimming towards him. The creature reportedly attacked him, but McClelland was able to fight it off with his fishing rod.

In 1963, a couple named James and Catherine Murray reported seeing the Dobhar-Chu while driving near Lough Mask. They claimed to have seen a large, otter-like creature with a dog-like head and a long, serpentine tail crossing the road in front of their car. The creature reportedly disappeared into the lake.

In the year 2000, an artist from Ireland named Sean Corcoran and his spouse asserted that they saw a Dobhar-Chu in a lake located in Omey Island in County Galway's Connemara region. According to Corcoran, the creature was big, had a dark complexion, and had orange flippers. Corcoran mentioned that "The creature" traversed the whole width of the lake from one end to the other in what seemed like only a few seconds." Finally, it jumped onto a large rock and disappeared, leaving behind a "most haunting screech," as described by Corcoran.

Despite the numerous reported sightings of the Dobhar-Chu, there has been little scientific evidence to support the existence of the creature. Many experts believe that the creature may be a myth or another example of the misidentification of other known animals. Otters, for example, are known to inhabit the waters of Ireland and can grow to be quite large.

Others believe that the Dobhar-Chu may be a surviving remnant of a prehistoric animal that once roamed the area. Some cryptozoologists have suggested that the creature may be a type of long-necked seal or a species of freshwater dolphin. Others claim that the Dobhar-Chu may also travel extensively, may inhabit many lakes around Ireland and could even be responsible for many of the world's 'lake monsters', including Scotland's Loch Ness monster, having followed humans as we immigrate between countries. Some also believe the creature *did* exist, but has long since gone extinct.

In recent years, there have been renewed efforts to investigate the legend of the Dobhar-Chu. In 2014, a group of scientists conducted a sonar survey of Lough Mask in an attempt to locate the creature. While the survey did not find any conclusive evidence of the Dobhar-Chu's existence, it did reveal several large underwater caves and tunnels that could potentially be hiding places for the creature.

Despite the lack of concrete evidence, the legend of the Dobhar-Chu continues to fascinate and intrigue people. It has become a popular subject of Irish folklore. The creature's fearsome reputation as a vicious predator has added to its allure, and many people continue to search for evidence of its existence or to catch one for themselves.

Winged Snakes

Old Swan Inn - Glamorgan

Glamorgan, or sometimes Glamorganshire, is a historic area of South Wales. The area has been inhabited by humans for over 200,000 years, with evidence of Neanderthals found in the Gower Peninsula. With an area having such a long history with humankind, it's no surprise there are also historic stories of people encountering strange things. One example would be the winged snakes.

The Winged Snakes of Glamorgan are mythical creatures that are said to inhabit the skies above the county of Glamorgan, in Wales. The creatures are often described as large, winged serpents that are capable of flying at great speeds. The legend of the Winged Snakes of Glamorgan has been a part of Welsh folklore ever since the first sighting.

The first recorded sighting of the Winged Snakes was reported in the early 1600s when a farmer in the area reported seeing a large, winged serpent flying through the sky. According to legend, the creature was so large that it was able to block out the sun. The farmer claimed that the creature had large, bat-like wings and a long, serpentine body that was covered in scales.

Over the years, there have been several other reported sightings of the Winged Snakes. In 1904, a group of farmers claimed to have seen the creature flying over their fields. They reported that the creature had a wingspan of at least 20 feet and was able to fly at great speeds. The farmers claimed that the creature had a long, thin body and was covered in shiny black scales.

Another famous sighting of the Winged Snakes occurred in 1922 when a pilot named Jack Phillips reported seeing the creature while flying his plane over the county. Phillips claimed that the creature had a wingspan of at least 50 feet and was able to fly at incredible speeds. He reported that the creature had a long, serpentine body and was covered in shimmering green scales.

In her 1909 book "Folk and Folk Stories of Wales", author Marie Trevelyan told a fascinating tale of a strange creature said to haunt a particular part of Wales. She said of the story, which was provided to her more than a century ago by a then-elderly, local woman: "The woods around Penllyn Castle, Glamorgan, had the reputation of being frequented by winged serpents, and these were the terror of old and young alike. An aged inhabitant of Penllyn, who died a few years ago, said that in his boyhood the winged serpents were described as "very beautiful."

Trevelyan continued: "They were coiled when in repose, and 'looked as if they were covered with jewels of all sorts. Some of them had crests sparkling with all the colours of the rainbow.' When disturbed they glided swiftly, 'sparkling all over,' to their hiding places. When angry, they 'flew over people's heads, with outspread wings, bright, and sometimes with eyes too, like the feathers in a peacock's tail.' He said it was 'no old story invented to frighten children,' but a real fact. His father and uncle had killed some of them, for they were as bad as foxes for poultry. The old man attributed the extinction of the winged serpents to the fact that they were 'errors in the farmyards and coverts.'"

Another such story also provided to Trevelyan, and also from the same area, states: "An old woman, whose parents in her early childhood took her to visit Penmark Place, Glamorgan, said she often heard the people talking about the ravages of the winged serpents in that neighbourhood. She described them in the same way as the man of Penllyn.

There was a 'king and queen' of winged serpents, she said, in the woods around Bewper. The old people in her early days said that wherever winged serpents were to be seen 'there was sure to be buried money or something of value' near at hand. "Her grandfather told her of an encounter with a winged serpent in the woods near Porthkerry Park, not far from Penmark. He and his brother 'made up their minds to catch one, and watched a whole day for the serpent to rise. Then they shot at it, and the creature fell wounded, only to rise and attack my uncle, beating him about the head with its wings.' She said a fierce fight ensued between the men and the serpent, which was at last killed. She had seen its skin and feathers, but after the grandfather's death, they were thrown away. That serpent was as notorious 'as any fox' in the farmyards and coverts around Penmark."

Despite the numerous reported sightings of the Winged Snakes around Glamorgan, as with all of these cryptids we are describing, there has been little scientific evidence to support the existence of the creatures. Some sceptics and experts suggest that the creatures may be a large species of bird, such as an eagle or a vulture.

Others believe that they may be a remnant of a prehistoric animal that once roamed the area. Some cryptozoologists have suggested that the creatures may be a type of pterosaur, a group of flying reptiles that lived during the time of the dinosaurs.

Some have also speculated that the Winged Snakes of Glamorgan may be a form of dragon, a creature that is deeply rooted in Welsh mythology. Dragons have long been associated with Wales, and many legends tell of battles between dragons and heroes. It is possible that the Winged Snakes of Glamorgan may be a modern incarnation of this ancient creature, serving as a reminder of the rich history and mythology of the region.

Black Dog Of Bungay

Bungay Market Town

"All down the church in midst of fire, the hellish monster flew, and, passing onward to the quire, he many people slew".

The tale of the Black Dog of Bungay, also known as Black Shuck, has been a long-standing legend in the small town of Bungay, located in the county of Suffolk, England. This eerie legend tells of a large, black dog that haunts the town and its surrounding countryside, appearing unexpectedly and causing misfortune to those who cross its path. The legend has been passed down through generations, and sightings of the black dog have been reported by locals and visitors alike. The descriptions of the beast vary in size and stature, ranging from that of simply a large dog to the size of a calf or even a horse. Some accounts of Black Shuck describe it as appearing headless, while others mention it as floating on a carpet of mist. Folklore states that the spectre haunts East Anglia's landscapes, primarily found in coastlines, graveyards, side roads, crossroads, bodies of water, and dark forests.

The first recorded sighting of the Black Dog of Bungay dates back to the 16th century, during a violent thunderstorm that caused the collapse of the roof of the local church. Legend has it that on August 4th, 1577, a large black dog burst through the doors of St. Mary's Church in Bungay to the sound of a loud clap of thunder. It ran up the nave, past a large congregation, killing a man and boy and causing the church steeple to collapse through the roof before moving on to Blythburgh Church, where it mauled and killed more people. Local accounts attribute the event to the Devil, with the scorch marks on the door of Blythburgh Church referred to by the locals as "the Devil's fingerprints," which can still be seen at the church to this day.

Over the years, many other reported sightings of the black dog have been made, both in the town of Bungay and the surrounding countryside. Many of these sightings have been associated with tragedy, leading to the belief that the dog is an omen of doom. Witnesses have claimed to have seen the creature wandering the countryside, while others have seen it lurking in the shadows of the town's narrow streets. In many cases, these sightings have been associated with some level of misfortune, with some witnesses claiming that they or someone they knew experienced a period of bad luck shortly after encountering the dog.

Despite the many reported sightings of the black dog, there is little agreement about what the creature actually is. Some believe that it is a supernatural being, sent to warn people of impending danger or to punish them for their sins. Others believe that it is simply a local legend passed down over the centuries and embellished with each retelling. There are also many theories about the origins of the black dog. Some believe that it is a remnant of the ancient pagan beliefs that were once prevalent in the area, while others think that it may be a manifestation of the devil or other malevolent forces.

In recent years, there have been fewer reported sightings of the Black Dog of Bungay, leading some to believe that the legend may be dying out. However, the legend still holds a powerful grip on the imaginations of many people in the town and surrounding area, and there are still those who claim to have encountered the creature. One of the most intriguing aspects of the Black Dog of Bungay legend is the fact that it has persisted for so many centuries. Despite the passage of time and the many changes that have occurred in the town and the surrounding countryside, the legend has remained an important part of the local folklore.

Today, the town of Bungay continues to celebrate its association with the Black Dog, with various events and attractions paying homage to the mythical creature. The Black Dog Running Club, for example, is a popular local sports club that takes its name from the legend, while the Black Dog Marathon is an annual event that attracts runners from all over the world.

Overall, the story of the Black Dog of Bungay is a testament to the enduring power of folklore and myth. Whether it is a supernatural being or simply a product of the human imagination, the legend has captured the hearts and minds of generations of people and is likely to continue to do so for many more years to come.

Black-Eyed Children

Cannock Chase

The Black-Eyed Children are a phenomenon that have been reported in various parts of the world, but perhaps the most famous sightings have occurred in and around Cannock Chase, a large area of forest in Staffordshire, England. These mysterious entities are said to be children with completely black eyes, who appear to be lost or in need of assistance. However, those who have encountered them report a sense of overwhelming fear and unease, and many believe that the Black Eyed Children are not what they appear to be.

The first reported sighting of the Black Eyed Children in the Cannock Chase area occurred in the late 1970s when a young couple were driving through the forest late at night. They reported seeing two children standing by the side of the road, one boy and one girl, both with completely black eyes. The couple offered to help the children, but they refused to speak and simply stared at them with their unsettling black eyes. The couple drove away in fear, and the incident was soon forgotten.

However, over the years, there have been many other reported sightings of the Black Eyed Children in and around Cannock Chase, leading some to believe that there may be something truly supernatural at work in the area. Some witnesses report seeing the children alone, while others have reported seeing them in groups. The children are said to be aged between 6 and 16 and are often described as having an old-fashioned appearance, and wearing clothes that are out of place in modern times.

One of the most famous and chilling stories of the Black Eyed Children in Cannock Chase occurred in 2013 when a woman named Tracy was walking her dog in the forest. She reported seeing two children, a boy and a girl, standing near a gate. The children appeared to be in distress, and Tracy approached them to offer help. However, as she got closer, she saw that their eyes were completely black, with no discernible iris or pupil. She immediately felt a sense of overwhelming fear and knew that something was not right. She quickly turned and ran away, and reported the incident to the local police.

Other reported sightings of the Black Eyed Children in Cannock Chase include encounters with groups of children who appear to be playing together in the forest, only to vanish without a trace when approached. Some witnesses have reported hearing strange noises, like the sound of children laughing, when there are no children in sight. Others have reported feeling a sense of unease or foreboding when passing through the forest as if they are being watched by unseen eyes.

A more recent sighting of this phenomenon came during the summer of 2021 when a couple were camping in Birches Valley. The teenage couple had been kept apart due to the coronavirus pandemic, so they planned to meet illegally in the forest. Due to this, their names have also been changed in all media about their sighting.

Around midnight, they heard sounds outside their tent, and assuming it may have been a deer, they stayed still and quiet hoping not to spook the animal. But once they heard footsteps, they unzipped the door and peeked outside. Both teenagers claimed to have heard the unmistakable sound of a little girl giggling, and so they turned on their torches trying to find the source of the sounds.

Then they saw something, running from tree to tree, hiding behind the trunks and peering out towards the couple before finally stepping out in front of them. The pair were terrified, having already heard stories of ghostly children in the area, and so they sat there, frozen, watching as this child got closer and closer.

They claimed it could "move in ways humans simply can't move. It was like it could teleport from one place to another when it was moving around and hiding behind the trees."

"I was shining my torch right at her and she just stood there staring at us with her head slightly dipped. That's when the giggling started to get louder and louder.

"It really sounded like it was coming from all around us even though I could see she was right in front of us. It was really disorientating for a few seconds.

"Then she bent down for a moment as if adjusting her shoes, stood back up, and ran off down a nearby path through a dense section of trees". The terrified pair then spent the night huddled together in their tent, waiting for sunrise.

Despite the many reported sightings of the Black Eyed Children in and around Cannock Chase, there is still much debate about what they actually are. Some people believe that they are the spirits of children who have died in the area, while others think that they are demons or other malevolent entities. Some sceptics suggest that the sightings are simply the result of overactive imaginations or misinterpretations of natural phenomena.

However, those who have encountered the Black Eyed Children report a sense of fear and unease that is difficult to explain. Many describe a feeling of being in the presence of something otherworldly, something that is not quite human. Some believe that the Black Eyed Children are a warning of some kind, a sign that something dark and sinister is lurking in the shadows.

There are also several anecdotal tales of other Black Eyed Children sightings around the world too, especially in the US. The stories vary slightly, with many involving suspicious "men in black" type figures seen in the vicinity of the children.

Cannock Chase itself is also home to many tales of the unexplained and paranormal. From its own bigfoot to werewolves, UFOs to spirits seen in WW2 uniforms, this area really does seem to have it all. If you are on the lookout for somewhere to have a strange experience, I couldn't recommend anywhere else more than Cannock Chase as a starting point.

Whatever the truth about the Black Eyed Children may be, there is no denying the fascination that they hold for those who have encountered them. They are a mystery that may never be fully explained, a haunting reminder of the strange and unsettling things that can happen in our world.

Speaking about Cannock Chase, we will be staying there for the next strange cryptid.

The Pigman

Cannock Chase

"When night falls, enter the woods at your peril, For inside lurks something worse than the devil. Avoid at all cost the gathering place, where at midnight the Pig-man roams on Cannock Chase...."

Cannock Chase itself is located in the West Midlands of England and is known for its natural beauty, wildlife, and obviously its mysterious occurrences. The Chase is also full of history. From the castle ring iron age hillfort to first world war camps. During recent surveys into the history of the area, prehistoric sites were even found. An area with such a long, rich history, will obviously help create many legends surrounding this forest.

One particular area of Cannock Chase, the Pye-Green Tower, seems to be a hotspot for these peculiar sightings. With UFOs, odd lights, werewolves, giant snakes, Bigfoot, black cats, aliens, and many reports of government officials sneaking around the perimeter of the tower and the forest. The tower was built during the Cold War as a backup communication system, as they were worried about an unexpected EMP attack from the Soviet Union. But some claim there is something more suspicious going on inside the tower.

Among the many legends and stories associated with the area, is that of the Pigman. The Pigman is said to be a half-human, half-pig creature that roams the woods of Cannock Chase.

Sightings of the Pigman date back several decades. Many who have reported seeing the creature describe it as standing between six and seven feet tall, with the body of a man and the head of a pig. Some say it has tusks, while others claim it has a human-like face with a pig's snout. Its fur or skin is said to be a dark brown or black colour.

The first recorded sighting of the Pigman was in the 1970s when a group of teenagers claimed to have seen it while camping in the woods. Since then, there have been numerous reports of sightings, with some people even claiming to have had direct contact with the creature.

One of the most well-known sightings of the Pigman was in 2007 when a man named Bob Wright claimed to have encountered the creature while walking his dog in Cannock Chase. Wright described the Pigman as being around seven feet tall and covered in dark fur. He said it had a human-like face with a snout and that its eyes were bright red. Wright claimed the Pigman was aggressive and tried to attack him and his dog before running off into the woods.

Another notable sighting of the Pigman occurred in 2014 when a group of hikers claimed to have seen the creature while walking through the woods at night. They described it as being around six feet tall, with a muscular body and the head of a pig. They said it was walking on two legs and appeared to be watching them before disappearing into the trees.

One expert on the paranormal goings-on in Cannock Chase is investigator and author, Lee Brickley. Lee has written books on the paranormal, with many of the stories based in the Staffordshire forest. After researching the mysteries of Cannock Chase for over a decade, Lee wrote the book; UFO's Werewolves & The Pig-Man: Exposing England's Strangest Location - Cannock Chase. In it, he shows some of the witness testimonies he came across during his research. One such sighting was sent to him via email, and it read as follows:

"Dear Mr Brickley,

I've seen something rather odd on Cannock Chase that I think may be of some interest to you. In October 1993, whilst walking around Castle Ring, myself and the wife heard some strange noises coming from the surrounding trees. Thinking it was likely to be a local couple enjoying an illicit liaison, we quickly moved away from the sound and headed back in the direction of our car. Upon reaching the steps down to the car park, I happened to turn around and lay my eyes on the strangest creature I've ever seen. This thing was seven feet tall, from the neck down it looked like a man, even wearing clothes, but its head was far too big for a human and it had an elongated face with a snout-like nose. When I pointed it out to my wife, she became terrified, so we started walking more quickly towards our car and got inside. That's when we started to hear this really high-pitched squealing noise that sounded like a pig being killed. That really spooked us....

Have you ever come across anything like this before?

Regards,

John & Anne"

While some dismiss the Pigman as nothing more than a legend or hoax, others believe that there may be some truth to the sightings. Some suggest that the creature may be a result of genetic experimentation or mutation, while others believe it may be a spiritual or supernatural entity.

Despite the lack of concrete evidence, sightings of the Pigman continue to be reported in Cannock Chase and the surrounding areas. While many may view the legend as a spooky tale, those who claim to have seen the creature describe it as a terrifying experience that has left them shaken.

The legend of the Pigman has also become a popular topic for paranormal investigators and enthusiasts. Many have conducted investigations in the woods of Cannock Chase, in an attempt to capture evidence of the creature's existence.

So what is the Pigman? Is it really a result of scientific experimentation? A supernatural entity? Or simply a spooky tale? Whichever it is, the legend of the Pigman adds to the mystique and intrigue of Cannock Chase, making it a place of fascination and wonder for visitors and locals alike.

The Owlman

Church at Village of Mawnan

For this creature, we are back in Cornwall, a county in the southwest of England. Cornwall is known around the world for its stunning natural scenery, rugged coastline, and rich history. It is also home to one of the most intriguing and mysterious legends in the country - the legend of the Owlman.

The Owlman is said to be a humanoid creature with the head of an owl and the body of a human. It is said to stand around six feet tall and has wings like those of an owl. The creature is said to have glowing red eyes that can hypnotise those who look into them.

The first reported sighting of the Owlman was in 1976 in the village of Mawnan, located on the Lizard Peninsula near St Mawnan and St Stephen's Church. Located about a mile from the village centre of Mawnan, the church is a peaceful building, surrounded by woods and boasting a breath-taking sea view. Two teenage girls, June Melling and Vicky Mawson, claimed to have seen the creature while walking through the woods near the church. They described the creature as being around five feet tall, with wings like those of an owl and a human-like body. The girls were reportedly so terrified by the encounter that they ran all the way home.

Since then, there have been numerous reports of sightings of the Owlman in and around Cornwall. Many of these sightings have occurred in the area around Mawnan and the nearby Helford River. Some people have reported seeing the creature flying over the river or perched on the branches of trees.

In 1989, a man named Brian Canham claimed to have encountered the Owlman while walking his dog in the woods near Mawnan. He described the creature as being around six feet tall, with wings like those of an owl and a human-like body. Canham claimed that the creature had glowing red eyes and emitted a strange, high-pitched screeching noise.

Some people believe that the creature may be a hoax or a misidentification of a barn owl or a large bird of prey. However, others believe that the Owlman may be a real, undiscovered species or a supernatural entity.

The legend of the Owlman has also inspired a number of theories and explanations. Some people have suggested that the creature may be an extraterrestrial or a product of genetic experimentation. Others have suggested that it may be a manifestation of ancient pagan beliefs or a spirit associated with the land, or connected to ley lines going beneath the nearby churchyard.

Many paranormal investigators and enthusiasts have conducted investigations in the woods around Mawnan and the Helford River, using equipment such as thermal cameras and audio recorders in an attempt to capture evidence of the creature's existence. Despite anecdotal claims of sightings and even people being attacked by this creature in recent years, unfortunately, these investigations are still to find concrete evidence of the owlman's existence.

Many people in the local area also seem to have forgotten about the owlman altogether. The few locals that do remember the original sighting, put this down to most of the older residents either passing away or moving and that the new younger population don't know anything about this myth.

There also seems to be a few similarities between the Owlman of Mawnan and Mothman (West Virginia, USA), and even the Manananggal (a cryptid found in the Philippines). They are all said to be part human, with wings, but are described as resembling different animal wings. Perhaps they are just misidentifications of the same creature, being found around the world? Or is that just one of the more popular creatures to hoax? Maybe one day we will find out.

The Beast Of Brassknocker Hill

Bretts Farm - Brassknocker Hill

The Beast of Brassknocker Hill is a mysterious creature that has been reported to roam the fields and woodlands around Brassknocker Hill, Bath, in the United Kingdom. There have been numerous sightings of the creature over the years, with some people claiming to have seen a large, black, panther-like animal, while others have reported a creature that is more like a hybrid between a wolf and a big cat. Some other witnesses have even claimed the creature was more like a bear.

The first reported sighting of the Beast of Brassknocker Hill dates back to the 1970s when a group of hikers reported seeing a large, black animal with piercing yellow eyes. The hikers claimed that the creature was at least four feet long and weighed around 150 pounds. They described it as being incredibly fast and agile, able to move through the underbrush with ease.

In July of 1979, locals Ron and Betty Harper discovered that bark had been ripped from their old oak tree by "an animal with teeth at least 20 times larger than the squirrels that usually inhabited the area." They claim that the region, which was usually full of birds and other wildlife, eventually grew mysteriously barren. Later that month, an eyewitness, who preferred to remain anonymous, claims to have seen the creature that had been causing all the damage. According to the report, the man was driving on a desolate stretch of road through Monkton Combe at night, when he encountered a bear-like creature, which was approximately 4 feet in length and bore two striking circular white rings around its eyes.

Since then, there have been many more sightings of the creature, with reports coming in from all over the area. Some people claim to have seen the creature at night, while others

84

have reported seeing it during the day. There have been reports of the Beast attacking livestock and pets, although there have been no reported attacks on humans.

One of the most famous sightings of the Beast of Brassknocker Hill occurred in 1984 when a man named Bill Stephens claimed to have seen the creature while walking his dog. According to Stephens, he was walking through a field near the hill when he heard a rustling in the underbrush. He turned to see a large, black animal with yellow eyes staring back at him. Stephens described the creature as being at least four feet long and weighing around 200 pounds. He said that it looked like a cross between a wolf and a panther.

Another notable sighting occurred in 1995 when a farmer named George Redpath claimed to have seen the Beast attacking one of his cows. According to Redpath, he was checking on his livestock late at night when he heard a commotion in one of the fields. When he went to investigate, he saw the Beast attacking one of his cows. Redpath claimed that the creature was incredibly strong and seemed to have no fear of humans. He fired his shotgun in the air to scare the creature away, but it didn't seem to have much effect.

Some people believe that the sightings of this creature are the result of misidentification or hoaxes, while others believe that the creature is a real, but elusive, animal that has managed to avoid detection for all these years.

One theory that has been put forward to explain the Beast's existence is that it is a black leopard. Black leopards are a rare mutation of the common leopard, and they are known to exist in some parts of the world, including Africa and Asia. While there have been no confirmed sightings of black leopards in the UK, it is possible that one or more of these animals could have been introduced into the wild at some point in the past. But this doesn't explain the 'bear-like' description given by one of the earlier witnesses. Others have put this down to the animal perhaps being some kind of skinwalker, a shapeshifting cryptid with the ability to be seen, or heard, as different creatures.

The Beast of Brassknocker Hill remains one of the most mysterious creatures in the UK, with sightings dating back over 50 years. While there is no conclusive evidence to prove its existence, the many reports of sightings and encounters suggest that there may be *something* out there in the fields and woodlands around Brassknocker Hill. Whether it is a real animal, a skinwalker or a figment of people's imaginations remains to be seen.

The Stronsay Beast

Stronsay Island

The story surrounding this cryptic creature goes back all the way to the early 1800s. The Stronsay Beast is a mysterious creature that has been the subject of much speculation and fascination for centuries. This strange sea creature is said to have washed up on the shores of Stronsay Island, located in the Orkney Islands of Scotland, in 1808. Since then, numerous sightings and reports of similar creatures have been recorded, sparking intense debate and discussion among researchers, scientists, and the general public.

The initial discovery of the Stronsay Beast was made by a group of sailors who were exploring the coastline of Stronsay Island. As they approached the beach, they noticed a large, strange-looking creature's carcass lying on the sand. It was described as being roughly 55 feet long, with a long, pointed head, and a series of sharp, jagged teeth. The creature's body was covered in matted hair or fur, and its overall appearance was said to be rather unsettling and frightening.

Upon closer inspection, the sailors noticed that the creature had a pair of large flippers, which seemed to indicate that it was some sort of sea creature. They also noted that the creature had a pair of gills on its neck, which suggested that it was a fish or some other type of aquatic animal.

News of the discovery quickly spread, and many people from around the area came to see the strange creature for themselves. Some even claimed to have seen similar creatures in the waters around Stronsay Island, sparking rumours and speculation about the possible existence of a sea monster.

The Natural History Society of Edinburgh could not identify the carcass and decided it must have been a new species, probably a sea serpent. Later, the anatomist Sir Everard Home in London dismissed the measurement, declaring it must have been around 36 feet, and deemed it to be a decaying basking shark (basking sharks can take on a 'pseudo plesiosaur' appearance during decomposition). In 1849 the Scottish professor John Goodsir came to the same conclusion. The largest reliably recorded basking shark was 40 feet in length, so at 55 feet in length, the Beast of Stronsay still constitutes something of an enigmatic cryptid.

Over the years, there have been numerous other sightings of similar creatures in and around the waters of Stronsay Island. Some have described the creatures as having a long, serpentine body, while others have reported seeing creatures with multiple tentacles or arms.

One of the most famous sightings of the Stronsay Beast occurred in 1900 when a group of fishermen reportedly caught a similar creature in their nets. The creature was said to be roughly 30 feet long, with a long, serpentine body and a series of sharp teeth. The fishermen were initially frightened by the creature but managed to capture it and bring it ashore. However, when they attempted to sell it to a travelling circus, the creature mysteriously disappeared, leading many to speculate that it was somehow related to the Stronsay Beast.

In the years since these initial sightings, there have been numerous other reports of similar sea creatures in the waters around Stronsay Island. Some have speculated that the creatures may be related to the legendary Loch Ness Monster.

Despite numerous sightings and reports, the true identity of the Stronsay Beast remains a mystery. Some have suggested that the creature may be a previously undiscovered species of sea creature, while others have speculated that it could be a giant eel or a type of giant squid.

What do you think of this story? Did the sailors stumble across the remains of a strange, cryptic creature from the depths of the ocean? Was it just a decomposing, and so less identifiable, commonly found animal, such as a basking shark? And will we ever find out the truth?

Cryptozoology - Honourable Mentions:

There are also many other cryptids in and around the UK, some have not been heard by many outside of a small group of locals. A lot of the more well-known cases also seem to describe a very similar, if not the same, creature.

But the most commonly found story in the UK seems to be that of mysterious wild cats, such as the Panther or a Puma. Below is a list of other famous sightings of creatures said to inhabit the UK, that have been described as the same as the other big cat sighting mentioned earlier, with a few details about the creatures and the sightings:

The Beast of Sydenham - Black, big-cat, Panther, the size of a labrador. Seen in Sydenham, London. 2002 - Present day.

The Surrey Puma - Black, big-cat, Puma. First seen around south-western Surrey. The 1960s - Present day.

The Beast of Dartmoor - Black/Beige, cat/dog, believed to have killed and injured livestock, 1988 - Present day

The Flintshire Puma - Black, Athletic-looking, Puma, Believed to have been spotted throughout North Wales, 2015 - Present day

So as we can see, there are a lot of big cat sightings around the UK. And those are just the ones the media have gotten a hold of and shared with a wider community. If we were to believe all of these sightings, it's safe to say we could all assume there is a rather large population of Puma or Panther-like big cats calling the UK countryside their home. If we look at how many sightings there have been in recent years around the UK of similar 'big cats', we see quite a large number of witnesses who claim to have seen these creatures:

The group Big Cats in Britain published reported sightings annually by county. The "top ten" counties or regions of Great Britain between April 2004 and July 2005 were:

Devon	Yorkshire	Scotland	Wales	Gloucestershire
676	127	125	123	104

Sussex	Cornwall	Kent	Somerset	Leicestershire
103	99	92	91	89

That all works out at 1600+ sightings across the UK, in a little over a year. That's A LOT of sightings for an animal that *doesn't* exist, and that experts claim doesn't have enough evidence.

Another big part of this puzzle, very often overlooked, are the number of reported big cats that have either been caught in live traps or killed in a number of ways from being shot to being accidentally hit by cars. They then went on to live in the local zoo/wildlife park and/or taxidermied and donated to local museums. These include A Canadian lynx shot in Devon in 1903, a puma captured in Inverness-shire, Scotland in 1980, two Jungle cats being hit by cars in separate incidents between 1988 - 1989 on Hayling island and Shropshire, and other incidents featuring Eurasian Lynx, Ocelot or Serval and a Caracal. So there is definitely evidence that there have been numerous big cats living wild in the UK countryside.

My personal belief is that while there are opportunities for people who want a big exotic cat as a pet, to get them into the country through smuggling, there will be those who then go on to release them in the wild when they are unable to control their pet or look after them correctly.

Shortly before this book went to publication, there were some huge developments in the question of the possibility of big cats in the UK. After a farmer in Gloucestershire noticed his second sheep in five years had mysteriously been killed, a crew filming a documentary called 'Panthera Britannia Declassified' investigated the possibility that the culprit behind the attack was a wild big cat. They discovered black fur stuck to a barbed wire fence and sent it off for DNA analysis. The forensic laboratory conducted the mitochondrial analysis and discovered a 99% match to a big cat species, most probably a black panther. This only further concretes the fact that these cats truly are out there, living in the British countryside.

But what about when it comes to the other cryptids mentioned in this book, do I believe they also exist?

I'm not a believer in any story that includes a 'devil' or 'demon', and I'm very sceptical of a story that has been told again and again, over decades or even centuries, knowing it could have been embellished or changed altogether. So this would put me on the more sceptical side of the argument.

But... I also have several theories about possible explanations for the paranormal, which include the possibility of extra dimensions to the universe. And if this was to be the answer for the paranormal, it could very well turn out to be an explanation for any of these cryptids, if not all of them. So I can't possibly say I don't believe it at all.

Perhaps I'll bump into the black-eyed children on one of my trips to Cannock Chase, and I will become a true believer. Although that will mean there will never be a Vol 2 of this book, as I will have been, literally, scared to death.

HAUNTINGS, GHOSTS & SPIRITS

Everything about ghosts, hauntings and spirits has long fascinated and intrigued people all over the world, and the United Kingdom is no exception. From ancient castles and historic houses and pubs to modern-day buildings and urban areas, the UK is said to be home to a plethora of haunted places, each with their own stories and legends. In this chapter, we will explore some of the most famous cases of 'paranormal activity' in the UK, and the evidence that supports its existence.

One of the most well-known examples of an apparent haunting in the UK is that of the Tower of London, which has a history spanning over 900 years. Visitors to the tower have reported sightings of ghostly apparitions, including the spirits of former prisoners and executed traitors, as well as the famous ghostly figure of Anne Boleyn, the second wife of King Henry VIII. The tower's famous resident ravens are also believed to be protectors of the tower, and their absence is said to signal its downfall.

Another famous case of a haunting in the UK is that of the infamous Enfield Poltergeist. This case gained worldwide attention in the late 1970s when a family in the London borough of Enfield claimed to be experiencing supernatural phenomena in their home. Witnesses reported seeing furniture move on its own, objects flying across the room, and even hearing voices coming from the walls. The case was investigated by paranormal researchers and sceptics alike, with some dismissing it as a hoax, while others remained convinced that something paranormal was at play.

In addition to these famous cases, the UK is home to countless other haunted locations, each with its own unique stories and legends. From the misty moors of Scotland to the bustling streets of London, and everywhere in between, ghostly sightings and paranormal phenomena continue to captivate the imaginations of people from all walks of life.

When looking into these locations, you will find that a lot of them claim to be 'the most haunted...', whether it be a pub, mansion, village, house, castle etc. When it comes to which location is more haunted than another, it's a very difficult thing to measure. Since the paranormal as a whole is something we don't truly understand, there is no way of knowing exactly how many ghosts etc call a certain location home. But as you will soon discover, this hasn't stopped the Guinness Book of Records from getting involved in some cases.

But what evidence is there to support the existence of ghosts and spirits? While sceptics may dismiss these phenomena as mere superstition and imagination, there have been many reported sightings and experiences that cannot be easily explained away. In the following pages, we will explore some of the evidence that supports the existence of ghosts and hauntings in the UK, and look at some of the possible explanations, both spooky and sceptical.

Pluckley Village - Kent

Church of St Nicholas - Pluckley Village

While deciding which case to start with, I figured where better to start than with a record-holding haunting. Pluckley Village, Kent is officially in the Guinness Book of Records, as the most haunted village in England, which it was awarded back in 1989. Once more well known for being the location for the 1990s television show, The Darling Buds of May, starring David Jason and Catherine Zeta-Jones, it is now world famous for its darker history. It is said to be home to between twelve and sixteen ghosts, spread around the whole village, some who are seen in one specific location, others that wander around the village, scaring locals and investigators alike.

Some examples of these ghosts are:

- The highwayman
- A phantom coach and horses.
- The ghost of a gypsy woman
- The Red Lady
- The White Lady
- The Miller
- The hanging body of a schoolmaster

With such an array of ghosts and spirits available, it is no wonder Pluckley Village is one of the most popular locations for ghost hunters, and those hoping to see something paranormal. Hundreds of investigators and enthusiasts make the trip to Pluckley every year in hopes of seeing something unexplainable and spooky. As you can probably imagine, Halloween is the most popular time for these visits, so if you're planning to go see this village for yourself, but don't want big crowds, I would suggest you choose another time of the year.

So let's have a look at some of these apparitions and the locations in which they can be seen.

We will start on the outskirts of Pluckley, in The Dering Woods. Known locally as 'The Screaming Woods', and reputed more widely as possibly being the most haunted woods in Britain (another possible record for the future). This eerie nickname comes from the numerous reports of blood-curdling screams coming from the woods at night, but there are also claims of footsteps and whispering being heard during the day.

The woods, which cover an area of approximately 300 acres, are also said to be home to numerous ghostly apparitions and unexplained phenomena. The legends and stories surrounding the Dering Woods have been passed down through generations, and they continue to fascinate and frighten people to this day.

According to the stories, the woods are haunted by the ghost of a highwayman who was pursued by villagers and eventually captured and killed in the woods. It is said that on certain nights, visitors to the woods can hear the screams and cries of the highwayman echoing through the trees. Others claim that the screams come from the ghost of a murdered woman who was buried in the woods.

There are also reports of a phantom monk who roams the woods at night, and sightings of a ghostly lady in white who is said to be searching for her lost child. Other paranormal activity reported in the woods includes ghostly apparitions, strange lights, and the feeling of being watched or followed by an unseen presence.

Despite the many stories and legends, there is no concrete evidence of any haunting in the Dering Woods. However, the eerie atmosphere of the woods, combined with the many reports of strange occurrences, has made it a popular destination for paranormal enthusiasts and thrill-seekers.

In 2008, a team of paranormal investigators decided to conduct an investigation of the Dering Woods. The team, led by paranormal researcher Richard Felix, set up equipment throughout the woods to try and capture evidence of any paranormal activity.

During their investigation, the team experienced a number of strange occurrences. They reported hearing unexplained footsteps and voices, and some members of the team claimed to have seen ghostly apparitions moving through the trees. The team also recorded several instances of electromagnetic interference, which they believed could be linked to paranormal activity.

Despite their experiences, the team was unable to capture any indisputable evidence of a haunting in the Dering Woods. However, their investigation did add to the legend and mystique surrounding the woods.

Since the investigation in 2008, reports of paranormal activity in the Dering Woods have continued. Visitors to the woods have reported hearing strange noises and feeling a sense of unease, while some claim to have seen apparitions moving through the trees. There have also been reports of unexplained lights and shadows, and others have reported feeling as though they were being followed or watched by an unseen presence.

In 2017, a different group of paranormal investigators conducted another investigation of the Dering Woods, this time using state-of-the-art equipment such as thermal imaging cameras and electromagnetic field detectors. The investigation yielded some interesting results, including several instances of unusual electromagnetic activity and the capture of strange, unexplained noises on audio recordings. If you're feeling brave enough, there are several paranormal tours that will take you through the screaming woods, some even offering you the opportunity to stay there overnight.

Moving on to the village itself. Located in Kent, UK, with a population just over one thousand people, there are an unusually high number of hauntings in such a small area. One of those ghosts is the Red Lady.

The Red Lady is one of the most well-known and frequently sighted ghosts in Pluckley Village. She is said to haunt the graveyard of St. Nicholas Church, where she can be seen wandering among the tombstones in her flowing red dress.

According to local legend, the Red Lady was a member of the Dering family who lived in nearby Surrenden Dering. She was said to be a beautiful woman, and she caught the eye of many suitors. However, she was in love with a man who was not approved by her family, and they forbade her from seeing him.

One day, the Red Lady's lover was killed in a tragic accident, and she was heartbroken. She fell into a deep depression and eventually died of a broken heart. Her ghost is said to have appeared shortly after her death, wandering through the graveyard in her red dress and mourning the loss of her beloved.

Over the years, there have been numerous sightings of the Red Lady in and around St. Nicholas Church. She has been seen wandering through the churchyard, standing beside her lover's grave, and even floating above the ground. Some witnesses have reported feeling a cold breeze or a chill in the air when the Red Lady is nearby, while others have heard her whispering or crying.

Despite the many sightings of the Red Lady, no one has been able to explain her appearance or why she continues to haunt the churchyard. Some believe that she is still mourning the loss of her lover, while others think that she is simply trapped in the earthly realm and unable to move on.

Her ghostly presence is a reminder of the village's past and the tragedies that have befallen its residents over the years. Whether you believe in ghosts or not, the sight of the Red Lady in her red dress is sure to send shivers down your spine.

The White Lady is another famous ghost that haunts the same churchyard. She is also said to appear in various locations throughout the village, including the nearby Screaming Woods and was seen in the library at Surrenden Dering House before it was destroyed by fire in 1952.

According to local legend, the White Lady was a woman who lived in the village in the 18th century. She was known for her beauty and her kind heart, and many of the local men were enamoured with her. However, our White Lady was already in love with a young man who worked in the watercress beds, and she refused to marry anyone else.

One night, her lover was killed in a freak accident in the watercress beds. She was devastated by the loss and spent many nights wandering the village in a white dress, mourning her beloved. Some say that she also searched for his ghost, hoping to be reunited with him in the afterlife. But I was unable to find any solid evidence of her life, or death, in Pluckley, so this may just be local storytelling.

However, over the years there have been many sightings of the White Lady in and around Pluckley Village. She is often described as a beautiful woman in a white dress, with long flowing hair and a sad expression on her face. One such witness who saw the spirit at the Surrenden Dering House was an employee of the US Embassy that used the building between WWI and WWII. He spent Christmas Eve performing an all-night ghost hunt, hoping to catch a glimpse of the woman seen wandering through the house. When he came face to face with the White Lady, he fired his rifle in fear, with the shot passing straight through her.

Even with the many sightings of the White Lady, her true identity and the reason for her haunting remain a mystery. Some speculate that she is still searching for her lost love, while others believe that she is simply unable to rest until she has found peace.

Despite the lack of unquestionable evidence, the legend of the Dering Woods, Pluckley village and their many apparitions continue to fascinate and intrigue people. Whether you believe in the paranormal or not, there is no denying that there is something eerie and mysterious about this area. I could write an entire book on just the spirits and ghostly goings-on in Pluckley, which shows this small village *really* does deserve its title as England's most haunted village.

The Enfield Poltergeist - London

284 Green Street - Enfield

As we started this section of the book with the most haunted village in England, the only way to follow that up is with the UK's (possibly the world's) most famous poltergeist case.

Enfield is a small suburb in North London, England. Most people around the world had never heard of Enfield, until the summer of 1977, when the area was thrust into the limelight due to claims of strange paranormal activity seen in the home at 284 Green Street.

In August 1977, the Hodgson family, which consisted of Peggy Hodgson and her four children, Margaret, Janet, Johnny, and Billy, began to experience strange occurrences in their home, including unexplained knocking and banging sounds, furniture moving on its own, and objects levitating. The family also reported hearing the voice of a man speaking in a gruff tone, which seemed to be coming from the walls.

As the activity continued, the Hodgsons became increasingly frightened and turned to the police for help. The officers who visited the home witnessed several instances of paranormal activity themselves, including furniture moving without explanation and toys appearing to be thrown across the room.

As the activity got more and more frequent, and subsequently even scarier for the family, the investigation of the Enfield Haunting eventually fell to two prominent paranormal investigators, Maurice Grosse and Guy Lyon Playfair. Grosse and Playfair spent many months at the Hodgson home, documenting the strange occurrences and attempting to find a rational explanation for the activity.

Over the course of their investigation, Grosse and Playfair witnessed and experienced several paranormal events that convinced them of the haunting's authenticity.

One of the most notable experiences was the voice of a man that seemed to be coming from the walls, and speaking through Janet. The investigators recorded several instances of this voice, which was later identified as belonging to Bill Wilkins, a previous tenant of the house who had died several years earlier. The voice spoke in a gruff tone and seemed to have a personal connection to Janet Hodgson, the daughter of the family.

The investigators also witnessed furniture moving on its own, toys being thrown across the room, and objects levitating. They reported feeling cold spots and seeing apparitions, including one of an elderly woman who appeared to be wearing Victorian clothing.

Perhaps the most infamous incident during the investigation was when Janet Hodgson was thrown across the room by an unseen force. The event was captured on film, and the photos became a focal point of the media coverage of the haunting.

Throughout their investigation, Grosse and Playfair attempted to find rational explanations for the activity they witnessed. They ruled out the possibility of hidden wires or other trickery, and they were unable to explain many of the events they witnessed.

Despite the sceptics who suggested that the Hodgson children were responsible for the hoax, Grosse and Playfair remained convinced of the authenticity of the haunting. They documented their experiences in a book, "This House is Haunted," which has become a seminal work in the field of paranormal research.

Other individuals who investigated the Enfield Poltergeist case included members of the Society for Psychical Research (SPR), a British organisation founded in 1882 to investigate paranormal phenomena. During the course of the Enfield investigation, several members of the SPR, including John Beloff, Alan Gauld, and David Robertson, visited the Hodgson family home to witness the phenomena firsthand and offer their own assessments. However, it was Grosse and Playfair who spent the most time with the family and documented the most extensive evidence of the haunting.

If you are a fan of horror movies, or more specifically, the Conjuring film series, you will no doubt remember many of these details from The Conjuring 2, directed by James Wan. In the film, the famous paranormal investigator couple, Ed and Loraine Warren visited the home and tried to help solve the case of what was really going on in Enfield. In the film, Ed and Loraine, after first believing the family to be making the whole haunting up for fame, decide to leave the house. They later realise that the voice of the old man speaking through Janet is actually just a pawn being used by the demonic nun character, who has since been given its own film in the Conjuring franchise. Ed and Loraine rush back to the house, to find Janet about to jump from a window to her death. Loraine speaks the name of the demon, given to her while she was in a trance, which sends the demon back to hell.

Now obviously most of that storyline was created to make the movie more dramatic. But Ed and Lorraine Warren did visit the Hodgson family home during the Enfield Poltergeist case, but they did not conduct a full investigation. They visited the house on two occasions and spoke with the family, but they were not involved in collecting evidence or conducting research on the phenomena.

However, the Warrens did later write about the case in their book "The Demonologist," and they described it as one of the most significant hauntings they had encountered. It is worth noting, however, that the Warrens' involvement in the case has been criticised by some researchers, who have accused them of exaggerating their role and misrepresenting the facts of the case. Claims that have only been exacerbated by the release of the film.

Possible explanations for the Enfield Haunting include poltergeist activity, a haunting by a malevolent spirit, or even a manifestation of the Hodgson children's own psychic abilities, which some believe could be triggered by children going through puberty and the change in hormones within their bodies, causing something to change in their minds, which then goes on to cause strange poltergeist-like activity.

Photos taken during the investigations, seemingly showing Janet being thrown by an unseen spirit, and voice recordings made during investigations by Grosse and Playfair can be found easily online, and do seem to show *something* strange going on.

Again, there are so many details to this fascinating case, I could go on and on. Do I personally believe the claims of the Hodgson family? I am not completely sold on the photos of Janet being 'thrown', as they could just as easily show her jumping off her bed. The strange voice talking through Janet could just as easily be caused by Janet herself manipulating her own voice.

But I also think that Maurice Grosse and Guy Lyon Playfair were very experienced investigators, and had no reason to just blindly believe the family and would not have been easily duped. Therefore, I would suggest finding those recordings and photos for yourself if you want to learn more about the Enfield Poltergeist, and you can make up your own mind.

Regardless of what you or I think of the case, it will always remain one of the most fascinating and controversial cases of paranormal activity in history.

Blickling Hall - Norwich

Blickling Hall

Blickling Hall is a stunning Jacobean mansion located in the picturesque countryside of Norfolk, England. With its grand architecture and rich history, it has become a popular destination for tourists and paranormal enthusiasts alike. But beneath its majestic appearance lies a dark and eerie history that has led many to believe that the hall is haunted by several ghosts.

The most famous of these ghosts is said to be that of Anne Boleyn, the second wife of King Henry VIII. Legend has it that Anne's father, Sir Thomas Boleyn, owned Blickling Hall at the time of her birth and that she spent much of her childhood there. In 1536, Anne was accused of treason and executed by beheading at the Tower of London.

It is said that on the anniversary of her death, her ghost returns to Blickling Hall, riding in a carriage drawn by a headless horseman, before entering the house and walking the halls in search of her lost child. Anne's ghost is often described as being dressed in a white gown, with her long hair flowing down her back.

Numerous sightings of Anne's ghost have been reported over the years, with many visitors claiming to have seen her walking the halls of the house or wandering through the gardens. Some have reported feeling a cold breeze or a sudden drop in temperature, while others have heard strange noises, such as footsteps or the sound of a carriage.

One of the most famous sightings of Anne's ghost occurred in the mid-19th century when a guest staying at the hall claimed to have seen her walking down the hallway towards him. He described her as being "very beautiful, with black hair, and wearing a white gown." He was so terrified by the encounter that he fled the house immediately.

Another famous sighting occurred in the 1930s when a group of guests were sitting in the library of the house. Suddenly, the door opened, and Anne's ghostly figure entered the room, walked towards the fireplace, and disappeared.

There have been many other reported sightings of Anne's ghost over the years, and it seems that her presence at Blickling Hall is still felt to this day, although usually limited to the anniversary of her death.

But Anne Boleyn is not the only ghost said to haunt Blickling Hall. There have also been reports of a spectral coach and horses galloping up to the front entrance of the house, as well as sightings of a ghostly woman wearing a brown dress who wanders the gardens.

And while Anne Boleyn is undoubtedly the most famous ghost said to haunt Blickling Hall, her father, Thomas Boleyn, is also believed to haunt the property. Thomas Boleyn was a prominent figure in Tudor England, serving as an ambassador to France and holding various positions in the royal court.

Legend has it that Thomas Boleyn's ghost appears at Blickling Hall in the form of a black dog. The dog is said to be a harbinger of death, and it is believed that anyone who sees the dog will soon meet their demise. The legend of the black dog is so well-known that it has become one of the hall's most enduring ghost stories.

There have been numerous reported sightings of the black dog over the years. Some visitors have reported seeing the dog wandering through the gardens, while others claim to have seen it inside the house. The dog is often described as being large and imposing, with glowing red eyes.

One of the most famous sightings of the black dog occurred in the 19th century when a coachman was driving his carriage past the hall. He saw the dog sitting in the road ahead of him and tried to swerve to avoid it. However, the dog vanished before he could hit it. The coachman reportedly died later that day.

Despite the legend of the black dog, there are some who believe that Thomas Boleyn's ghost may appear in other forms as well. Some visitors have reported seeing the ghostly figure of a man walking through the gardens or the hall's corridors. The figure is often described as wearing Tudor-era clothing, which is consistent with Thomas Boleyn's time period, and carrying his own head under his arms.

Over the years, several paranormal investigations have been carried out at Blickling Hall. In 2002, the British paranormal investigation show "Most Haunted" filmed an episode at the hall, which aired on national television. The show's presenters reported feeling an eerie presence in the house and captured several unexplained phenomena on camera, including orbs of light and strange noises.

Blickling Hall has been the subject of numerous paranormal investigations over the years. Many paranormal groups and ghost hunters have visited the hall to try and capture evidence of the reported hauntings. One of the most comprehensive investigations took place in 2015 when a team of paranormal investigators spent several nights at the hall.

The team set up cameras and recording equipment throughout the house, hoping to capture evidence of the reported hauntings. They also used a variety of other paranormal investigation tools, such as EMF metres and thermal cameras, to try and detect any unusual activity.

During the investigation, the team captured several interesting pieces of evidence. One of the most compelling pieces of evidence was a series of photographs that showed what appeared to be an apparition of a figure in the library. The figure was described as being a woman dressed in a white gown, which is consistent with the description of Anne Boleyn's ghost.

The team also captured several EVPs (Electronic Voice Phenomena) during the investigation. These are recordings of voices that are not audible to the human ear but can be detected using recording equipment. Some of the EVPs captured at Blickling Hall were described as being "clear and distinct," and appeared to be in response to questions asked by the investigators.

Despite the compelling evidence captured during the investigation, some sceptics remain unconvinced. They argue that the evidence could be explained by natural phenomena or could have been faked by the investigators. However, many believe that the evidence provides further proof of the reported hauntings at Blickling Hall.

The investigations at Blickling Hall continue to this day, with many paranormal groups and enthusiasts visiting the house to try and capture evidence of the reported hauntings. If you wish to attend this location, hoping to experience this paranormal activity for yourself, you can visit the hall during the day, and the building is run by the national trust.

You can also find several paranormal tours that will take you around the building after dark and will go into more detail about the spirits said to reside there and strange sightings experienced by previous tours. If you are hoping to see the ghost of Anne Boleyn, 19th May is the anniversary of her death and the date on which she is said to appear.

So, who are these ghosts that are said to haunt Blickling Hall? While some may dismiss them as mere legends or tales, others believe that there is a deeper truth to their existence. It is possible that the spirits of those who lived and died at the hall still linger there, unable to move on to the next world. Or perhaps the hall's rich history and reputation for being haunted have created a kind of energy vortex that attracts paranormal phenomena.

Whatever the explanation may be, one thing is certain: Blickling Hall is a place of great beauty and intrigue, but it is also a place where the lines between the living and the dead seem to blur. Those who dare to venture into its hallowed halls may, perhaps, find themselves face-to-face with the ghosts that call it home.

Pendle Hill - Lancashire

Pendle Hill

Now we move further north in England, from Norfolk to Lancashire, to one of the most famous places in the UK among ghost hunters and paranormal investigators.

Pendle Hill has long been associated with stories of witchcraft, dark magic, and paranormal activity. The area has a rich and haunting history that dates back centuries, making it a fascinating location for those interested in the paranormal.

Perhaps the most well-known aspect of Pendle Hill's history is the infamous witch trials that took place in 1612. The trials centred around a group of twelve people, mostly women, who were accused of practising witchcraft and conspiring to murder. The trials were a product of the intense fear and paranoia that existed at the time, with many people believing in the existence of witches and their ability to bring harm to others. The Pendle Witch Trials of 1612 are considered to be one of the most significant events in English history related to witchcraft.

The most famous of the accused were two women named Elizabeth Southerns (also known as "Demdike") and Anne Whittle (also known as "Chattox"). Both women were well-known in the area for their supposed powers of witchcraft, and their families had a long-standing feud with each other.

The accused were tried at Lancaster Castle, which was known for its harsh treatment of prisoners. The trial was presided over by Judge James Altham, who was known for his belief in the existence of witches. The prosecution relied heavily on the testimony of a young girl named Jennet Device, who claimed to have witnessed the accused practising witchcraft. Jennet was the granddaughter of Elizabeth Southerns and was also a key witness against her own mother and brother, who were also among the accused.

The trial lasted for several days, and the accused were not given proper legal representation. They were eventually found guilty, with ten of them being executed by hanging. The trials have since become a significant part of English history and have helped to shape the way we think about witchcraft and the supernatural. They were widely reported in the press, and many people became even more afraid of witches and their supposed powers.

The trials also led to changes in the legal system, with greater emphasis being placed on the use of evidence and proper legal representation. In 1736, the Witchcraft Act was passed, which made it a crime to claim to have magical powers or to accuse someone else of witchcraft.

Today, the Pendle Witch Trials are remembered as a dark chapter in English history, a time when fear and superstition led to the persecution of innocent people.

Pendle Hill is said to be haunted by the spirits of those accused and executed during the witch trials. Visitors to the area have reported strange sightings, including ghostly apparitions, mysterious lights, and unexplained noises. Some people claim to have felt a sudden drop in temperature while walking through the area, suggesting the presence of an otherworldly force.

There are also reports of a ghostly figure known as the "White Lady," who is said to wander the area in search of her lost child. Legend has it that the White Lady was one of the accused witches who was executed during the trials.

In addition to the ghosts of the accused, there have been reports of other paranormal activity in the area. Some visitors have claimed to have seen strange lights hovering in the sky, while others have reported feeling a sense of unease or dread while walking through certain parts of the hill.

Pendle Hill's reputation for paranormal activity has attracted the attention of many investigators and ghost hunters over the years. These individuals have come to the area in an attempt to capture evidence of ghostly activity and communicate with the spirits of the accused witches.

One such team of investigators visited the area in 2014 and spent several nights conducting investigations at various locations, including the Pendle Hill Witches Trail and the Lancaster Castle dungeons where the accused witches were held.

During their investigation, the team claimed to have captured several pieces of evidence that suggest the presence of supernatural activity. They captured footage of strange noises and unexplained lights, and they also claimed to have seen the ghostly apparition of a woman in a white dress, who they believed to be the "White Lady" associated with the area.

Other paranormal investigators have reported similar experiences. Some have claimed to have captured images of ghostly figures on camera, while others have reported feeling a sense of unease or dread while walking through certain parts of the hill.

In addition to using cameras and other equipment, some investigators have conducted séances in an attempt to communicate with the spirits of the accused witches. These sessions involve a group of people gathering together and attempting to contact the dead through mediums or other spiritual practices.

Some of these séances have reportedly been successful, with participants claiming to have received messages from the spirits of the accused witches. However, others have been less successful, with no apparent communication taking place.

In 2004, the popular television show "Most Haunted" aired a special live episode on Halloween from Pendle Hill. The episode was watched by millions of viewers, and it remains one of the most infamous and controversial episodes in the show's history.

The "Most Haunted" team, led by paranormal investigator Yvette Fielding, spent the night in the shadow of Pendle Hill, conducting a series of investigations in some of the area's most haunted locations. The episode featured psychic mediums, historians, and other experts, who were all tasked with trying to uncover the truth about the ghosts and supernatural phenomena associated with the area.

As the night wore on, the team experienced a number of strange and unsettling occurrences. One of the most notable incidents involved the controversial psychic medium, Derek Acorah, who claimed to be in contact with the spirits of the witches who were executed at Pendle Hill. Acorah became visibly upset and began to make strange noises and movements, which some viewers interpreted as evidence of possession.

Other team members reported seeing ghostly apparitions, hearing unexplained noises, and feeling sudden drops in temperature. At one point, Yvette Fielding herself claimed to have been pushed by an unseen force, causing her to fall to the ground.

As the night progressed, tensions ran high, with some team members feeling genuinely scared. The show ended with no conclusive evidence of the supernatural, leaving viewers to draw their own conclusions about what had happened.

The "Most Haunted" episode at Pendle Hill remains controversial to this day, with some critics claiming that the show relied too heavily on dramatic effects and staged activity.

However, for many fans of the paranormal, it remains a classic and spine-chilling example of the kind of unexplained phenomena that can occur at haunted locations.

Despite the claims made by paranormal investigators, many people remain sceptical of the existence of ghosts and other supernatural phenomena. Some argue that the experiences reported by investigators can be easily explained by natural phenomena, such as wind or shadows.

Others suggest that the legends and stories associated with the area are simply a result of a rich and haunting history, rather than actual evidence of paranormal activity.

While the existence of ghosts and other supernatural phenomena remains a matter of debate, there is no denying the unique and eerie atmosphere of Pendle Hill. The area's association with witchcraft and the paranormal has made it a popular destination for those interested in the supernatural, and it will likely continue to intrigue and fascinate people for years to come.

Pendle Hill is arguably one of the UK's most haunted locations, but it will also serve as a reminder of a dark part of our history, which I feel it is important to remember and learn from.

Borley Rectory - Essex

Borley Rectory - 1892

Borley Rectory, located in the village of Borley in Essex, England, was once described as "the most haunted house in England". The history of the rectory is a fascinating one, filled with mystery, intrigue, and tragedy.

The original Borley Rectory was built in 1863 on the site of an old monastery. It was a large, Gothic-style building that quickly became the centre of village life. The first reports of paranormal activity at the rectory came in the late 1800s when the residents of Borley began to report strange noises and ghostly apparitions in and around the house.

Eric Smith and his wife lived in the rectory for a short while and claimed to have heard doorbells ringing on their own, mysterious footsteps and poltergeist activity. They contacted the Daily Mirror newspaper, who contacted Harry Price and asked him to investigate.

Price's investigations uncovered evidence of past tragedies at the site, including a nun who had fallen in love with a monk. The pair had tried to elope together but were found and were both sentenced to death. The monk was reported to have been sent to the gallows and the nun was said to have been bricked up alive in the walls of the monastery. The spirits of both are now claimed to be seen around the rectory.

Price also discovered that the previous owner of the rectory, who had been a reclusive and unpopular figure, had committed suicide by shooting himself in the head.

Despite Price's investigations, the paranormal activity at the rectory continued unabated.

After several unsuccessful attempts to exorcise the building, Mr and Mrs Smith moved out.

The next residents were Reverend Lionel Foyster and his wife Marianne. Almost immediately, they began to experience the same strange phenomena. Objects would move on their own, doors would open and close by themselves, and ghostly figures would appear in the hallways. The poltergeist activity was also said to have become more aggressive, with Mrs Foyster being thrown from her bed by something unseen.

The Foysters moved out of the house after five years, which left Price to move in and continue his investigation uninterrupted. Unfortunately, Harry Price and his team of researchers experienced much fewer examples of either ghostly or poltergeist activity. Harry then went on to write a book on his findings during the long investigation of Borley Rectory, called 'The Most Haunted House in England'.

The rectory was demolished in 1944 after being badly damaged in a fire. Today, the site is marked by a plaque that commemorates the history of the house and the many paranormal phenomena that occurred there.

In the decades since the demolition of Borley Rectory, the house has become a cultural touchstone for ghost hunters and paranormal enthusiasts. Many books have been written about the history of the house, and it has been the subject of numerous documentaries and TV shows.

Obviously, this location is also a beacon for paranormal investigation teams and tours. In 2015, a team of paranormal researchers conducted a thorough investigation of the site.

This team used a range of advanced equipment, including infrared cameras, digital voice recorders, and electromagnetic field (EMF) detectors, to try and capture evidence of paranormal activity at the site. Over the course of several nights, the team explored the grounds of Borley Rectory and conducted a series of experiments to try and communicate with any spirits that may be present.

During their investigation, the team reported a number of unusual occurrences, including cold spots, unexplained noises, and sightings of ghostly apparitions. They also captured several pieces of footage that they believe show evidence of paranormal activity, including a strange mist that appeared to move across the room and a shadowy figure that appeared to be standing in one of the windows of the rectory.

Despite this continued interest, the true nature of the haunting at Borley Rectory remains a mystery. Some believe that the paranormal activity was caused by the tragic events that occurred on the site, while others believe that the house was cursed by some unknown force.

Me personally? I believe there may have been something going on at Borley Rectory, and even that some of the poltergeist activity was really happening. Perhaps the activity slowed down once the Foysters moved out as they could have actually been triggering some kind of reaction from the spirits of the nun and the monk. Is it *still* haunted? Well if you believe popular theories, especially the theory on residual hauntings, this would mean that energy from those who once lived and died at this location could have been imprinted on the earth at the site of the rectory. This would mean, even though it was demolished, the ghosts would still be visible, wandering around as if it were still the 1800s.

If you are interested in experiencing the strange occurrences at Borley Rectory, there are several groups that run tours all year round. They will guide you around the site, some will be accompanied by the group's resident psychic and many have the technology for you to use throughout the investigation.

Ancient Ram Inn - Gloucestershire

Ancient Ram Inn

The Ancient Ram Inn is located in Wotton-under-Edge, a small market town in the county of Gloucester, and it is another great example of a building with a very long history of paranormal goings on. It is thought to date from around 1145, is believed to have been built on top of an ancient pagan burial ground and has housed workers, priests and more before being converted into an inn. The last pint was pulled there in 1968.

After it had closed its doors, John Humphries purchased the building from the brewery and intended to turn it into a quiet family home. But he soon realised, he wasn't alone in the house.

The ghosts that are said to haunt the Ancient Ram Inn include a number of spirits from different periods in history. One of the most famous ghosts is that of a young girl who is said to have been murdered in the building many years ago. Her ghost has been seen wandering the corridors and rooms of the inn, and visitors have reported feeling a cold chill in the air when she is near.

Another ghost that is said to haunt the Ancient Ram Inn is that of a monk. The ghost is believed to be the spirit of a monk who was hanged on the site in the 16th century. Visitors have reported seeing the ghostly figure of a monk walking through the inn, and some have even claimed to have heard the sound of his footsteps echoing through the building.

Other ghosts that are said to haunt the Ancient Ram Inn include a malevolent presence that is said to make people feel uncomfortable and uneasy. This ghost is believed to be the spirit of a witch who was burned at the stake on the site, and her ghost is said to be particularly active in one of the upper rooms of the inn.

The Ancient Ram Inn has been investigated by many paranormal researchers over the years, and there have been countless reports of strange occurrences and unexplained phenomena. Visitors to the inn have reported hearing strange noises, seeing ghostly apparitions, and feeling a cold chill in the air. The building has also been the site of many ghostly sightings and encounters, with some visitors claiming to have been physically touched by the spirits that haunt the inn.

John Humphries also claimed to have been attacked by a succubus during his time at the inn. According to Humphries, the succubus was a female demon that would visit him in the middle of the night and try to seduce him.

Humphries described the succubus as having long hair and piercing eyes, and he claimed that she would appear to him in his bed as he slept. The demon would crawl up his body and attempt to have sex with him, draining his energy and leaving him feeling weak and exhausted.

Humphries claimed that the attacks by the succubus continued for many years, and he eventually sought the help of a psychic medium to try and rid the inn of the demon. The medium performed a cleansing ritual in the room where Humphries had been attacked, and after that, he claimed that he was no longer bothered by the succubus. Many visitors to the inn, however, have reported feeling a strange presence in the room where Humphries was attacked, and some have even claimed to have seen the succubus herself.

However, sceptics point out that the story of the succubus may have been exaggerated or even fabricated by Humphries in order to increase the inn's reputation as a haunted destination. Regardless of whether the succubus is real or not, the story has become a popular part of the legend of the Ancient Ram Inn.

Moving away from the paranormal for a second, there are many other very strange happenings at the Ancient Ram Inn. During an investigation, a diviner told Humphries that there were children buried all over the place at his family's home. John decided to dig, and when he did he found piles of bones and daggers buried together under his floor, which he assumed was evidence of sacrificial killings.

Caroline Humphries, John's daughter, spoke to the Mirror newspaper in Feb 2022 about the findings. Caroline, 60, said: "There was an archaeological report on the daggers and they said the dates of them are undefined but they were 'of a great age'. Sadly the daggers, which were in a glass display case, were stolen around 2014 when my father was in the house, showing a group of visitors around. They will be of great value and because of the scribblings on them, they could be linked to ritualistic killings".

John took the bones to a specialist who was convinced they were not animal bones. John also discovered a 500-year-old mummified cat inside one of the walls during some renovation work. The cat was in remarkably good condition, due to lime render in the walls, and the family believed it had been placed there to protect the home from witches.

In more recent times Caroline's partner Mick has also discovered bones including a jaw, spine, femur bones, and a skull.

The settlement and buildings surrounding the Inn are believed to date back to at least 900 AD or older. It's believed to have once housed slaves, Catholic monks, and stonemasons who built the local St Mary's Church. Caroline also believes there is a hidden cellar and passageway under the house leading to the nearby St Mary's Church. She explained: "The caveat in the deeds from Whitbreads from when we bought it states that the building's cellars have been bricked up but we still don't know where they are."

The Ancient Ram Inn remains a highly contested location, with sceptics and believers alike hotly debating the authenticity of its ghostly inhabitants. Despite this, the inn continues to attract visitors from all over the world, eager to explore its dark history and experience its haunted reputation for themselves.

Whether you believe in ghosts or not, there is no denying that the Ancient Ram Inn is a fascinating and eerie place. Its history is rich and storied, with tales of murder, witchcraft, and the supernatural. And while some of the stories may be exaggerated or even fabricated, there is no denying the profound effect that the inn has had on those who have experienced it firsthand.

For many, the Ancient Ram Inn is a place of mystery and intrigue, a site where the veil between the living and the dead seems to be especially thin. For others, it is simply a curious relic of England's past, a building steeped in history and legend.

For me, it's a very old building with a long interesting history, and buildings that are older and have seen a lot more human activity, seem to be the home of much more paranormal activity. So this does match very well with much-believed theories about what ghosts are, and why they are found in certain locations. Whatever your own beliefs, there is no denying the allure of the Ancient Ram Inn, a place where the boundaries of the natural and supernatural worlds blur, and the past and present collide.

Chillingham Castle - Northumberland

The North Front - Chillingham Castle

Chillingham Castle is located in the northern part of England and has a long and dark history that dates back to the 12th century. The castle is famous for its ghostly encounters, and it is believed that it is one of the most haunted castles in England. Over the centuries, many ghost stories have emerged about the castle, and it has become a popular destination for ghost hunters and paranormal enthusiasts.

Chillingham Castle was built in the 12th century and was initially used as a fortress to defend against Scottish raids. Over the centuries, the castle has been the site of many battles and sieges.

During the 16th century, the castle was converted into a family home and underwent several renovations. However, its dark past never truly faded away, and the castle became known for its legends of ghostly encounters.

During World War II, the castle was used as a military hospital and housed wounded soldiers. After the war, the castle fell into disrepair until the 1980s, when it was purchased by Sir Humphry Wakefield, who restored the castle to its former glory.

Today, Chillingham Castle is open to the public, and visitors can take guided tours of the castle and its grounds. The castle is also available for private events and weddings and even has rooms to hire so you can spend the night hoping for a glimpse of one of its many resident spirits.

The most famous of those spirits is the "Blue Boy." The legend of the Blue Boy has fascinated visitors for centuries. According to the legend, the young boy was the son of the Earl of Tankerville, who lived at the castle in the 17th century. The boy was said to have been caught stealing and was locked in a room as punishment. However, the room was not properly ventilated, and the boy died of suffocation.

Since then, visitors to the castle have reported seeing the ghostly figure of a young boy wearing blue clothing wandering the halls of the castle. Some claim that he appears as a misty blue figure, while others say that they have seen him in vivid detail.

One famous story involves a group of soldiers who were stationed at the castle during World War II. They were playing a game of cards in the Pink Room when they suddenly heard a loud banging on the door. When they opened the door, they found nothing but an icy cold breeze. Later that night, they saw the ghostly figure of a young boy in blue standing at the foot of their bed.

Over the years, many theories have been put forward to explain the legend of the Blue Boy. Some believe that he was the illegitimate son of one of the castle's residents, while others think that he was simply a servant boy who met a tragic end. Sightings of this particular spirit did stop for a while, after the bones of a child, surrounded by decaying fragments of blue cloth, were found behind a wall. These remains were given a proper Christian burial, and the spirit of the Blue Boy was thought to have left the castle, that was until the room began being let out, and then visitors reported seeing bright blue flashes shooting from the walls.

Another well-known ghost is that of Lady Mary Berkeley. She was a former resident of the castle who died in the 18th century.

According to legend, Lady Mary's ghost has been seen in the castle's chapel, where she kneels in prayer. Visitors have reported hearing strange noises and seeing the ghostly figure of a woman in a long, flowing dress.

Lady Mary's story is a tragic one. Her husband, Lord Grey, ran away with her sister, leaving Mary alone with just her young daughter for company. It is said that she became increasingly lonely and depressed, which may have contributed to her untimely death.

Lady Mary's ghost is said to be a benevolent spirit, and many visitors report feeling a sense of peace and comfort in her presence. Some even claim to have seen her smile or heard her voice speaking to them. Her haunting presence adds to the eerie atmosphere of the castle and serves as a reminder of the tragic history that lies within its walls.

Today, Lady Mary's ghost is a popular subject for ghost hunters and paranormal enthusiasts. Her story has been featured in many books and documentaries, and her haunting presence continues to draw visitors to Chillingham Castle from all over the world.

The White Pantry Ghost is another spirit that is said to haunt the castle and it is one of the oldest and most enduring ghost stories associated with Chillingham Castle. According to legend, this ghost is that of a servant who was caught stealing from the castle's pantry by the castle's owners. As punishment, she was bricked up in the pantry and left to die, sealing her fate as a tragic ghost forever trapped within its walls. Visitors claim to have seen her ghostly figure in the pantry, and some have reported hearing her cries for help.

Many visitors to the castle have reported experiencing strange phenomena around the pantry. Some have heard strange whispers and cries for help, while others have felt an eerie coldness in the air. Some even claim to have seen the ghostly figure of the White Pantry Ghost herself, a pale and ethereal presence who seems to be forever trapped within the castle's walls.

While the story of the White Pantry Ghost may be just a legend, it has become an integral part of the folklore and haunted history of Chillingham Castle.

The Haunted Dungeon is also a popular spot for ghost hunters. This dungeon was used to hold prisoners, and it is said that the screams of the tortured souls who were held there can still be heard today. Visitors to the dungeon have reported feeling cold spots and hearing strange noises.

Whether you believe in the haunting, or you're more sceptical, there is no denying the eerie atmosphere that surrounds this ancient fortress. I, for one, will definitely be checking into the castle for a night or two, hoping to see the Blue Boy or Lady Mary. Perhaps I'll see you there.

Berry Pomeroy Castle - Devon

Berry Pomeroy Castle

Berry Pomeroy Castle is a ruined castle located in Devon, England, with a reputation for being one of the most haunted castles in the country. Berry Pomeroy Castle was built in the late 15th century by the Pomeroy family. The castle changed hands several times over the centuries and was eventually abandoned in the 18th century. The castle has a dark and turbulent history, with many tragic tales of love, betrayal, and murder. It is said that the spirits of the castle's former residents still haunt its ruins. Today, the castle is a popular tourist attraction, and its ruins serve as a chilling reminder of the dark and often tragic history of the castle and its former residents.

The most famous ghost at Berry Pomeroy Castle is the White Lady, who is said to haunt the castle's dungeons. According to legend, the White Lady is the ghost of Margaret Pomeroy, the daughter of one of the castle's former owners. Margaret's sister, Eleanor, was jealous of her beauty and imprisoned her in the dungeons, where she eventually died. Visitors claim to have seen the ghostly figure of the White Lady wandering the dungeons, and some have reported feeling her icy breath on their skin.

Another ghost that is said to haunt Berry Pomeroy Castle, is the Blue Lady. The stories surrounding the Blue Ladies' origins seem to differ quite a lot depending on the source. Some claim she may have been the daughter of a Norman lord and is said to wander the dungeons mourning the loss of her baby, which she murdered as it was sired by her own father. Others claim that she was a servant who fell in love with one of the castle's owners but was tragically killed by his jealous wife. Others suggest that she was a former resident of the castle who died under mysterious circumstances.

Visitors claim to have seen her ghostly figure in the Great Hall, wearing a blue dress and staring mournfully out of the window. It is also claimed that she beckons visitors to the tower, and if they go to her, they mysteriously fall to their death. Despite the many different legends surrounding her ghostly presence, the Blue Lady remains one of the most enduring and haunting figures associated with Berry Pomeroy Castle.

While the White Lady and the Blue Lady are the most well-known ghosts at Berry Pomeroy Castle, there are other spirits said to haunt the ruins as well. Among these are the ghosts of two brothers who are said to have leapt to their deaths from one of the castle's towers.

According to legend, the two brothers were both in love with the same woman. Unable to resolve their differences peacefully, they climbed to the top of the tower and jumped together to their deaths. Their tragic end has left an enduring mark on the castle, and their ghosts are said to still haunt the tower to this day.

Visitors to the castle have reported seeing the ghostly figures of the two brothers on several occasions. Some have reported hearing their ghostly cries and screams echoing through the castle, while others have reported feeling a sense of unease and sadness in the vicinity of the tower where they met their end.

Another example of paranormal sightings is of a spirit that is said to haunt the castle's chapel. The ghost is reported to be that of a young boy who was murdered by his own brother. Visitors claim to have heard the ghostly sounds of the murdered brother crying and calling out for help in the chapel.

The Soldier is yet another ghost that is said to haunt Berry Pomeroy Castle. According to legend, the Soldier is said to have died during the English Civil War. Visitors claim to have seen his ghostly figure in the castle's courtyard, wearing a red coat and carrying a musket.

Over the years, a number of investigations have been conducted, and some have yielded intriguing findings.

One of the most famous investigations of Berry Pomeroy Castle was conducted in 2005. During their investigation, the team reported hearing unexplained noises, feeling cold spots, and seeing strange lights and shadows. They also captured some intriguing footage of what appeared to be a ghostly figure moving across the Great Hall.

In 2009, another paranormal investigation was conducted by a team hoping to capture evidence of the spirits living here. Using a range of equipment, including electromagnetic field detectors and temperature sensors, the team attempted to capture evidence of ghostly activity. While they did not find any conclusive evidence of paranormal activity, they did report feeling a sense of unease and heaviness in certain areas of the castle, particularly in the dungeons and chapel.

In 2016, a group of paranormal investigators conducted a night-time investigation of Berry Pomeroy Castle. During their investigation, they reported hearing strange noises, including footsteps and voices and captured some intriguing footage of what appeared to be ghostly orbs floating around the castle's ruins.

Other investigators claim to have caught photographic evidence of the spirits of the two brothers, with the photos supposedly showing the ghosts of two horses and riders.

While the findings of these investigations may be open to interpretation, they serve to add to the intrigue and mystery of Berry Pomeroy Castle.

The castle's ruins offer a glimpse into a bygone era, and its many legends and ghost stories continue to fascinate visitors. Whether you believe in the paranormal or not, a visit to Berry Pomeroy Castle is sure to be a memorable and spine-tingling experience.

Samlesbury Hall - Lancashire

Samlesbury Hall

Samlesbury Hall, located in the picturesque countryside of Lancashire, England, is a 14th-century manor house filled with history and mystery. With its stunning architecture and beautiful gardens, it has been a popular attraction for tourists and history enthusiasts alike.

However, what many visitors don't know is that the hall is also home to some of the most intriguing paranormal activity in the country.

The history of Samlesbury Hall dates back to 1325 when it was built by Gilbert de Southworth, a wealthy landowner. Over the centuries, it has been owned by several prominent families, including the Harringtons and the Crosse family, who made significant alterations and additions to the building and the surrounding manor. It was also involved in another of England's infamous witch trials, with three women, known as the Samlesbury witches, accused and later acquitted of witchcraft.

Today, it is managed by the Samlesbury Hall Trust, a non-profit organisation that is dedicated to preserving the hall's history and ensuring that it remains open to the public.

However, the hall's long and storied history has also left its mark in the form of supposed ghosts and hauntings. The most famous of these is the White Lady, who is said to haunt the Great Hall of the building.

There are several theories about the identity of the White Lady ghost, but one of the most popular is that she is the spirit of Dorothea Southworth. Dorothea was the daughter of Sir John Southworth, who owned the Hall in the 16th century.

According to legend, Dorothea fell in love with a young man who was visiting the Hall. The young man was a member of a rival family and was a Protestant, whereas her family were devout Catholics. Therefore their love was forbidden, and Sir John was furious when he discovered their relationship and ordered Dorothea to end it immediately.

But Dorothea and her lover refused to obey Sir John's orders and continued to see each other in secret and planned to run away together. However, one day, Dorothea's lover was caught by her own brothers, who brutally attacked the boy and killed him on the spot.

Dorothea was then sent to a nunnery where, heartbroken by her loss, she is said to have died of grief shortly after her lover's death. Her ghost has been seen wandering the Great Hall ever since.

Another famous ghost is that of a young boy, who is said to have drowned in the nearby River Ribble. His ghost is often seen playing in the gardens of the Hall, and some visitors have reported hearing the sound of children's laughter coming from the area.

There are also reports of a ghostly monk who haunts the hall's chapel. It is believed that he is the spirit of a former resident of the Hall who was a member of a religious order. Visitors have reported seeing the monk walking through the chapel, as well as hearing the sound of his footsteps and chanting.

One of the most intriguing aspects of the paranormal activity at Samlesbury Hall is that it seems to be concentrated in certain areas of the building. For example, the White Lady is said to only appear in the Great Hall, while the ghostly monk is only seen in the chapel. This has led some paranormal investigators to speculate that there may be some kind of residual energy or psychic imprint that is attached to certain parts of the building.

Another haunting story associated with Samlesbury Hall, and probably my favourite for this location, involves a priest who died in the building in the 16th century. According to legend, the priest was caught celebrating Mass in secret during a time when it was illegal to do so. He was discovered by the authorities and arrested, and it is said that he was tortured and killed in the Hall.

There are several reports of paranormal activity associated with the priest's death. Visitors to the Hall have reported feeling a sense of unease or even terror in the area where the priest is said to have died. Some have even reported hearing strange noises or whispers that cannot be explained.

But perhaps the most chilling aspect of the story is the bloodstained floorboards in the Hall that are said to be impossible to clean. According to legend, no matter how many times the boards are scrubbed or sanded, the bloodstains always return. Some believe that this is because the spirit of the priest is still trapped in the Hall, unable to rest until his death has been avenged.

The bloodstained floorboards have become a popular attraction for ghost hunters and paranormal investigators over the years, with popular shows such as Ghost Hunters International, amongst others, investigating the location. In 2004, the crew from the popular UK TV show, Most Haunted, visited Samlesbury Hall to conduct a paranormal investigation.

The team reported a number of strange occurrences during their investigation. They claimed to have captured images of shadowy figures moving through the Hall and to have heard unexplained noises and voices on their EVP recordings. Some members of the team even reported feeling physical sensations, such as sudden drops in temperature and the feeling of being touched or grabbed by unseen hands.

One of the most notable moments of the investigation came when Yvette Fielding and a cameraman claimed to have seen the figure of a woman in a white gown standing at the top of the stairs. This figure has been identified as the White Lady.

Despite the dramatic events captured on camera during their investigation, some viewers of Most Haunted have criticised the show for its use of special effects and for being overly sensationalistic in its approach to ghost hunting. However, there is no denying that the show's visit to Samlesbury Hall helped to bring attention to the building's haunting history and to fuel interest in paranormal investigations.

Despite the many reports of paranormal activity at Samlesbury Hall, the current owners of the building are quick to point out that they do not actively promote or advertise the building as a haunted attraction. Instead, they prefer to focus on the hall's rich history and architecture, while acknowledging the role that the paranormal has played in its legacy. Although I will note that ghost tours are still available to book year-round.

There is no denying that Samlesbury Hall is a fascinating and enigmatic place. With its stunning architecture, beautiful gardens, and rich history, it is a true treasure of Lancashire. But is it a haunted treasure? Or are these nothing but legends and tall tales? Perhaps the only way to know is to visit for yourself.

Buckland Abbey - Devon

"Take my drum to England, hang et by the shore, strike et when your powder's runnin' low, If the Dons sight Devon, I'll quite the port o' Heaven, An 'drum the up the Channel as we drummed them long ago." - Sir Henry Newbolt 1895

Buckland Abbey, located in Devon, UK, has a rich and intriguing history that dates back to the 13th century. Originally built as a monastery for the Cistercian Order, the abbey has gone through several transformations throughout the centuries, from a Tudor mansion to a farmhouse and eventually becoming a National Trust property in the 20th century.

Despite its centuries-long history, Buckland Abbey is perhaps best known for its numerous ghostly sightings and hauntings. Many visitors and employees have reported unexplained phenomena, ranging from cold spots and strange noises to apparitions and full-bodied manifestations.

One of the most famous ghosts at Buckland Abbey is that of Sir Francis Drake, the famous Elizabethan sailor, and explorer who purchased and lived at the abbey during the 16th century. According to legend, Drake rebuilt the abbey in just three nights, as he invoked the help of the devil himself. The story goes that because he made a deal with Lucifer, Drake's spirit is said to still haunt the grounds, dressed in his trademark hat and cloak. and sometimes accompanied by a pack of hell-hounds. Visitors have reported seeing his apparition wandering the grounds or standing at the window of his former bedroom. Drake's famous drum also resides here, and he supposedly gave instructions that it was to be returned to Buckland Abbey as he lay dying aboard his ship off Puerto Bello, Panama, in January 1596. It is

170

believed that the spirit of Drake lives in this drum and that the beating of which will be heard whenever England is in trouble. It was heard on the eve of the battle of Trafalgar and again in 1939 when Europe was on the verge of WWII.

Another well-known ghost is that of a monk, who is often seen walking through the gardens and along the abbey's corridors. Some believe that he may be the spirit of a former monk who was executed during the dissolution of the monasteries under Henry VIII. There have also been reports of a lady in white, who is said to wander the halls of the abbey and occasionally appear at the top of the staircase.

One particularly chilling account involves a group of National Trust employees who were working late one night. As they were leaving, they noticed a figure standing at the end of the hallway. The figure appeared to be a monk, and as they approached, it vanished into thin air. The employees were so frightened that they refused to return to the abbey after dark.

The National Trust has even embraced the abbey's spooky reputation, offering ghost tours and special events throughout the year. For those who are brave enough to explore its halls and gardens, Buckland Abbey offers a unique and unforgettable experience, blending history and legend in equal measure.

Felbrigg Hall - Norfolk

Felbrigg Hall

Felbrigg Hall, located in Norfolk, UK, is a stunning 17th-century country house with a long and intriguing history. The estate the hall is located on was originated by the Felbrigg family, and they owned the estate until Sir Simon de Felbrigg died in 1442, and then it was passed down to the Norfolk Windhams. But when that family line died, it was passed to the Somerset Wyndham family. It was first given to John Wyndham and it then stayed with his family for centuries.

Since then, the hall has undergone several renovations and changes of ownership, before being acquired by the National Trust in the 20th century.

During the 18th century, the estate underwent major renovations under the ownership of William Windham II. He transformed the manor house into a grand country house with a magnificent hall, drawing room, and dining room. Later on, the estate passed to William Windham III, who was a well-known politician and literary figure. He was a close friend of Samuel Johnson and was a member of the Literary Club, which included some of the leading literary figures of the time.

William Windham III was a patron of the arts and had an impressive collection of paintings, books, and antiquities. He was also a keen agriculturalist and is credited with introducing new agricultural techniques to the estate.

During World War II, the estate was used as a training ground for the Royal Air Force, and the house was used as a hospital for wounded soldiers. After the war, the estate was acquired by the National Trust, and it has been open to the public since the late 1960s.

Despite its idyllic setting and picturesque appearance, Felbrigg Hall has long been associated with paranormal activity. Many visitors and employees have reported strange occurrences, ranging from inexplicable noises and cold spots to full-blown apparitions and unexplained movements.

One of the most well-known ghosts at Felbrigg Hall is that of William Windham III who died in 1810. Windham is said to haunt the library, where his portrait hangs and is often seen sitting in his favourite chair, reading a book. Some visitors have even reported the scent of tobacco smoke, which is believed to be associated with Windham, who was a known smoker.

Another ghost that has been reported is that of a maid, who is said to have been murdered by her master in the 18th century. Her ghost has been seen wandering the halls of the house, carrying a candle, and is often accompanied by the scent of lavender.

There have also been reports of a ghostly presence in the Queen Anne room, where a figure is sometimes seen standing at the window, looking out over the gardens. The room is also known for its unexplained cold spots, and some visitors have reported feeling as though they were being watched.

Then there are the ghosts of the sisters, Gertrude and Marion Ketton, who lived in the hall from 1863 when their father purchased the property. They later lived there with their older brother, who inherited the hall when their parents died. The sisters took great care of the hall, with gardening and interior design as just some of their hobbies. The latter would be their cause of death. Arsenic was used as a green pigment in paint and wallpaper, especially the shades Paris Green, Emerald Green, Scheele's Green, and Schweinfurt Green. These were also very popular during this time and the sisters' love of interior design would have seen them keep up with trends. Gertrude Ketton died on July 20, 1895, and her sister Marion died three years later on April 5, 1898. The spirits of the girls have been seen wandering around the halls and the gardens, tending to their flowers.

Felbrigg Hall has a lot to offer, if you're interested in the paranormal or not. With beautiful gardens and grounds, 380-acre woods, a tea room and a second-hand book store, there is a lot to keep you entertained during a daytime visit. But if you, like me, are more interested in seeing one or more of these spirits, there are ghost tours available to book through several companies that offer a guided walk around the building and will explain more about the history, the spirits who call the property home and where you are likely to see them.

Felbrigg Hall truly is a remarkable example of a historic English country estate, and its rich history and fascinating stories have captivated visitors for generations. From the grand architecture of the house to the beautifully landscaped gardens, every corner of Felbrigg Hall is steeped in history and mystery.

St Briavels Castle - Wye Valley

St Briavels Castle

St Briavels Castle is a fascinating historic site located in the heart of the Wye Valley in Gloucestershire, England. The castle has a long and storied history, dating back to the 12th century, and is known for its haunting tales and ghostly sightings.

The castle was originally built by William the Conqueror in 1067 as an iron forge. Later this was seen as an important royal castle, with the surrounding Forest of Dean used as the king's hunting grounds. The building was later converted into a debtors' prison in the 13th century. During this time, it was used to house prisoners awaiting trial in nearby Gloucester.

The castle was also used as a courthouse, and several notable trials were held there, including the trial of the notorious Judge Jeffreys in 1685.

Over the years, the castle has been the site of many gruesome events, including murders and acts of treachery. It is believed that the spirits of those who suffered and died at the castle continue to haunt its halls to this day.

With such a long and rich history, going back around a thousand years, it is no wonder this castle appears to have so much activity, with each room seemingly filled with different ghostly goings on.

The cries of a baby can be heard in the 'Solar Room'. To make these sounds even creepier, during restorations to the ceiling in this room, the wrapped-up remains of a baby fell from the rafters. Even though the remains were removed, the cries can still be heard.

Another perfect example of residual haunting is the ghost of the Knight in full armour that can be seen standing where the castles keep used to stand. He can be seen standing perfectly still, guarding the castle, as the light from the full moon reflects off the shiny surface. His ghost is then said to disappear. The fact that the castle's keep is no longer there, and yet the spirit appears where it stood, means to most investigators that his energy has been imprinted on the stone surrounding it, and under the right circumstances, it is seen as a sort of projection. These kinds of spirits are obviously not able to communicate with investigators as it is not believed there is any more than energy left there.

The main type of activity this castle appears to get is auditory, with the sounds of objects being dropped/moved, laughing, screaming or doors being slammed. The 'hanging room' is a great example of this, with strange sounds such as marbles dropping, humming, and scuttling noises often heard in this room. Witnesses also claim to have seen a dark, shadowy figure standing in the doorway and have even claimed to have been violently pushed by some unseen force.

There are also claims of poltergeist activity here, in the prison, with furniture being moved and people being "grabbed" by something unseen. The sounds of voices, footsteps and even growling have also been heard here. Other claims of activity in other rooms of the castle vary from sounds, strange sights, and physical experiences. They include people witnessing indentations on their beds as if someone is sitting down, the sudden feeling of lightheadedness and strangulation, strange unexplained rustling noises and overbearing putrid smells, and in the 'Porters Lodge' a gentleman staying at the castle reported being pinned down on his bed, with feeling as if he was unable to move.

But if you are hoping to stay at this castle to experience something strange for yourself, may I suggest staying in the 'Oubliette. This room is home to the "scary bed". Guests who spend the night in this bed have woken up in the night to a woman screaming, and something violently tugging on the bed sheets, seemingly angry that they are in the bed. St Briavels Castle seems to be a very good place to start if you want to experience something truly unexplainable.

The castle has been beautifully restored and is now used as a youth hostel, offering visitors a unique and memorable overnight experience. Whether you're a history buff, a ghost hunter, or simply looking for a unique and atmospheric place to visit, St Briavels Castle is a must-see destination that is sure to leave you with a sense of awe and wonder.

Whitby Abbey - Whitby, Yorkshire

Whitby Abbey

Whitby Abbey is an iconic landmark in the coastal town of Whitby, Yorkshire. Founded in the 7th century, the abbey has a long and fascinating history that is steeped in legend and lore. It is known for its many ghostly sightings and paranormal activity.

The abbey was originally founded as a monastery by Hild, the daughter of an Anglian nobleman, with the support of the Northumbrian king Oswiu in 657 AD. Over the centuries, it grew in size and influence, becoming one of the most important religious centres in England. However, in the 16th century, it was dissolved by King Henry VIII as part of the Dissolution of the Monasteries.

Despite its dissolution, Whitby Abbey continued to play an important role in English history. During the 18th and 19th centuries, it became a popular destination for tourists and artists, who were drawn to its stunning Gothic architecture and dramatic cliff-top location.

However, the abbey's ghostly reputation also grew during this time. Visitors reported seeing apparitions of monks and nuns, as well as phantom soldiers and ghostly sailors.

One of the most famous ghostly sightings at Whitby Abbey is that of a phantom horse and carriage that is said to race across the abbey's grounds at night. Legend has it that the carriage is driven by the devil himself and that those who see it are cursed with bad luck.

Another famous ghost is that of a young girl who is said to haunt the museum. The girl is believed to have died in a fire at the abbey, and her ghost has been seen playing with toys and laughing in the museum's exhibits.

Other reported sightings include the ghost of a monk who walks along the abbey's walls, a headless ghost who wanders the grounds, and the spirit St Hilda, who founded the abbey at Whitby, is said to be seen peeking from the highest windows of the ruined castle.

There are also several cryptid-type creatures said to call the abbey, and the surrounding area, home. There is the muscular, dog-like beast, most commonly referred to as The Barghest, along with stories of creatures referred to as Boggarts or Boggles, but more commonly known as a Hob. The Barghest legend has it that The Barghest stalks its prey on the North Yorkshire Moors surrounding Whitby and that it preys on farmers' livestock and wild animals, using its jet-black fur to blend in with the night. The fact a huge black dog running up the steps to the abbey was mentioned in Bram Stoker's Dracula has only added fuel to the story of this strange beast.

The Hob is a type of small mischievous goblin-like creature, thought to call the caves around Whitby home. There is a lot of legend surrounding these hob-goblins, primarily that these creatures are very bad-tempered and like nothing more than to move into somebody's house and cause chaos. It is also believed that once a Hob has decided to move into your home, they are almost impossible to remove. They have been known to damage property, turn milk sour and frighten livestock. Some believe, however, that these creatures were made up by smugglers who used the caves to store their goods, hoping to ensure that no one wandered in and found their stash.

Despite its haunted reputation, Whitby Abbey remains a popular tourist destination, and visitors can explore its ruins and learn about its rich history and the many ghostly tales that surround it. The abbey has also been featured in numerous works of literature, including Bram Stoker's Dracula.

Bram Stoker's iconic novel, Dracula, is a masterpiece of Gothic literature that has captured the imaginations of readers around the world for over a century. While the novel is set in Transylvania and England, it is believed that Stoker was inspired by his visit to the coastal town of Whitby, where he stayed in 1890.

During his stay in Whitby, Stoker is said to have been struck by the town's dramatic coastline and the imposing ruins of Whitby Abbey, which overlook the town from a clifftop perch. It is believed that Stoker drew on these images and the town's spooky atmosphere to create the eerie landscape of Dracula.

In the novel, the character of Dracula arrives in England aboard a ship that crashes near Whitby. He then takes up residence in a house overlooking the town and the abbey ruins. This location closely resembles Stoker's own lodgings during his visit to Whitby.

It is also believed that Stoker was inspired by local legends and folklore surrounding the abbey and the town's history. These stories included tales of shipwrecks and sea monsters, as well as legends of ghosts and vampires.

Whitby Abbey itself features prominently in Dracula, serving as the location of several key scenes in the novel. The abbey's ruined state and eerie atmosphere provide the perfect backdrop for the novel's Gothic themes, and it has become an iconic part of the Dracula mythos.

Whether you're a fan of horror literature, a history buff, or simply looking for a unique and atmospheric place to visit, Whitby and its famous abbey are sure to captivate and inspire you.

Tower of London - London

The Tower of London

The Tower of London is one of the most well-known places around the world. The British royal family and all of their estates attracted over 737 thousand visits by tourists between April 2021 and March 2022 and they are estimated to be worth £1.7 billion in revenue. After Buckingham Palace, one of the most visited places in London is the Tower of London.

Originally built in the 11th century by William the Conqueror, the Tower of London has served various purposes throughout its long and storied history. It has been a royal palace, a prison, a treasury, and a zoo, among other things. But perhaps the most famous aspect of the Tower of London is its reputation for being haunted. There are said to be 13 ghosts that call this famous building home, and with the building's history, it's no wonder there is so much unexplainable activity going on here.

Over the centuries, the Tower of London has been the site of numerous executions and acts of violence. Visitors and staff alike have reported hearing strange noises, feeling sudden drops in temperature, and seeing apparitions of figures from the past.

One of the most famous ghost stories associated with the Tower of London is that of Anne Boleyn. Anne was the second wife of King Henry VIII and was executed at the Tower in 1536 for treason. It is said that her ghost has been seen walking the grounds, often with her head tucked under her arm. Some have also reported hearing her disembodied voice crying out in the night.

Another famous ghost said to haunt the Tower is that of Sir Walter Raleigh. Raleigh was a poet, explorer, and courtier who was imprisoned in the Tower for 13 years. It is said that he can still be seen wandering the halls of the Tower, smoking his pipe and reciting his poetry.

One of the Tower's most gruesome ghosts is that of the so-called "Princes in the Tower." The Princes were two young boys, Edward V and his brother Richard, who were imprisoned in the Tower in 1483 by their uncle, the future King Richard III. They were never seen again and are believed to have been murdered. Their ghosts have been seen wandering the Tower, often accompanied by the sound of their plaintive cries. When the bones of two small boys were found under the stairs in 1674, most people believed them to be the missing princes and the bones were given a royal burial at Westminster Abbey.

Other ghosts reported to haunt the Tower include that of Lady Jane Grey, the "Nine-Day Queen" who was executed in 1554, and of the Countess of Salisbury, who was executed in 1541.

There are many other ghosts, some who are known, including royalty, and some just given the names "Grey Lady" and "White Lady". These include Henry VI, Lord Guildford

Dudley, Arbella Stuart, Guy Fawkes, and even animals have been witnessed.

The sounds of animals, such as monkeys and lions, have been heard over the years but the apparent spirit of one was seen by a guard on duty. The guard claimed that a Grizzly Bear charged at him and, defending himself, he attempted to kill the animal with his bayonet. The sword seemingly passed straight through the bear, which then vanished. The guard was left confused and making little sense and was carried to his room, where he died two days later.

Despite the many reports of ghostly sightings, the Tower of London is still used for official ceremonies and events. It is also home to the Crown Jewels, which are on display for visitors to see.

Whether or not you believe in ghosts, a visit to the Tower of London is sure to leave a lasting impression on anyone who ventures within its walls. If you are ever to visit this famous location, there are several tours a day that explain in much more detail who died at the tower and who is said to still walk the halls.

Aston Hall - Birmingham

Aston Hall - Birmingham

Aston Hall is a stunning Jacobean mansion located in the heart of Birmingham, England. Built in the 1600s by Sir Thomas Holte, the hall was home to the Holte family for over 200 years. Today, the hall is open to the public as a museum, and it is known not only for its impressive architecture and historical significance but also for its ghostly inhabitants.

Throughout its long history, Aston Hall has had its fair share of tragedies and scandals. One of the most famous incidents occurred in the mid-17th century when the Hall was attacked by Parliamentary troops during the English Civil

War. The oak staircase still shows the scars from this time.

One of the most famous ghosts at Aston Hall is said to be the spirit of the daughter of Sir Thomas Holte, Mary. Legend tells of Holte's obsession with his status, and that he ruled over his family like a dictator. When his young daughter planned to elope with the man that she loved, and Halte disapproved of, he locked Mary in her bedroom for the next sixteen years. She eventually went mad and died in the room. Visitors have claimed to see and hear the young girl, known now as the Grey Ghost, asking to be freed.

Another of the ghosts at Aston Hall is that of the White Lady. She is said to be the ghost of Lady Holte, who died in the 18th century. Lady Holte was known for her beauty and her love of the Hall, and it is said that her ghost still wanders the house. Many visitors have reported seeing her figure in the corridors or in the gardens surrounding the Hall.

Another ghostly inhabitant of Aston Hall is a former servant girl named Elsie, also known as the Green Lady. Details surrounding Elsie and her life and death only seem to come from paranormal investigators using tools such as spirit boxes, but they claim she died tragically in the hall's kitchens, and her ghost is said to have remained behind. Many visitors have reported feeling a cold presence in the kitchens, and some have even reported seeing Elsie's apparition. She is sometimes even mistaken for a member of modern-day staff and visitors have asked her for help or information, only for her to vanish.

There are also claims of the spirit of a young house boy named Dick, who hung himself after being accused of stealing.

There have also been reports of a ghostly child at Aston Hall. The child's identity is unknown, but many believe that it could be one of Lady Holte's children. The child's ghost is said to be mischievous, and visitors have reported hearing laughter and footsteps in the hallways.

Aston Hall is now open to the public for tours, so be sure to get yourself there if you would like to hopefully catch a glimpse of one of its resident spirits.

Station Hotel - Dudley

Station Hotel

The Station Hotel in Dudley, West Midlands, is a grand Victorian building that has stood for over 100 years. Originally built as a hotel for railway travellers, and frequented by many celebrities including George Formby, Bob Hope, and Laurel and Hardy when they were staring at the theatre across the road from the hotel. But despite its many uses, the Station Hotel is now perhaps best known for its ghostly inhabitants.

There have been many reports of paranormal activity at the Station Hotel over the years. One of the most famous ghosts is that of a former chambermaid who is said to have died in one of the hotel rooms. Her ghost has been seen by many guests, often appearing as a translucent figure standing at the foot of the bed or sitting in the chair close to the window. Some guests have reported feeling a cold presence in the room and hearing strange noises during the night. She is also often accompanied by the ghost of a small child, who has been seen sitting and even jumping on the beds, even while visitors are sleeping in them. Both spirits have been seen to wander through the walls, from one room to another.

There have been numerous paranormal investigations of the Station Hotel, but perhaps the most famous of these would be the filming of an episode of Most Haunted. During this visit by the TV crew and hosts, accompanied by psychic Derek Accorah, they appeared to encounter many of the spirits that call this hotel home. Derek reported the name George Williams/Williamson and claimed it to be the name of a male spirit who was once the hotel manager. He then claimed that George had been having an affair with a female barmaid by the name of Elizabeth Hitchen.

Derek then claimed that George enticed the girl down to the cellar after she had threatened to tell his wife of their affair, where he strangled and stabbed the poor girl to death. He went on to tell of how he disposed of her body, using a chute that would have been used for the delivery of bottles and barrels, and then buried her in the street outside. Accorah then claimed that her body is still there to this day. Others have changed some of the details of this story, claiming, as nobody has ever been found, that perhaps he put her body inside a barrel and it was taken away with the next collection by the brewery. There are also claims that George was arrested for her murder, but unfortunately, due to the displacement of historical records, many of these claims are difficult to back up.

Derek Accorah also claimed to see the spirit of a man named George Lawley, who he claimed knew of the murder and wrote about it in a ledger. The ledger was unfortunately never found, but it does appear that a local historian, named George Lawley did in fact write for the brewery at the time.

Accorah then went on to describe the spirits of two young children also at the hotel. Catherine aged 6/7 died under the wheels of a carriage and Richard aged 3/4 passed away after a blood-related illness.

This is where I will add one of my own personal paranormal experiences. More specifically, of one of my son's experiences. Around December 2018, I was driving my family back home and we were taking our usual route which takes us past the Station Hotel. I live less than 6 miles from the hotel, so I wasn't too far from home.

My son, Charlie, would have been around three at the time and as we were sitting at a red light, with the front of the hotel in view, this was the conversation we had:

"Mommy, that girl is sad."

Confused, me and my wife start looking around on the street and in nearby cars, wondering who he meant.

"She's sad because her mommy is angry at her, isn't she Mommy."

At this point, we have no idea what he's talking about and decide to humour him and see what else he says. So my wife asks where the girl is he was talking about.

"She's in the road. She was playing in the road, and her mommy told her not to play in the road, but she did and she got hurt, and now her mommy is sad."

Now we are really confused, still looking around to see if there is an injured girl in the road that needs help or something similar. But we still can't see anything, so we ask where he can see her and if he can see her mom.

"She's outside that building" (he points to the Station Hotel) "and her mommy is in the window upstairs, looking at her and crying."

At this time, we knew the reputation the hotel had of being haunted, so we joked that maybe he had seen one of the ghosts. It wasn't until we got home and checked the history of ghost sightings at the hotel that we learned about Catherine, the girl who supposedly died under the wheels of a cart while staying at the hotel. We tried asking Charlie more questions about the girl he saw, but at this point, he had lost interest and did not want to answer them. But in our minds, he had already said enough to corroborate the story of Catherine's death and haunting of the Station Hotel. It also added validity to the claims that many people make that children can see things that we cannot see.

In addition to these ghostly figures, there have been reports of strange noises and unexplained events throughout the hotel. Doors have been known to open and close on their own, and objects have been moved without explanation. Many guests have reported feeling a sense of unease in certain parts of the hotel.

The Station Hotel is no longer the must-stay hotel it once was, but it is still a popular location for locals. It is one place I must personally recommend you stay, after our strange experience. If you do go and stay, or even just drive past, and you see Catherine, please get in contact and let me know. I would love to have more evidence of her haunting at this location.

Eyam - Derbyshire

The village of Eyam in Derbyshire

Eyam, also known as the plague village, or the village of the damned, is a picturesque village nestled in the heart of the Derbyshire countryside. It is known not only for its stunning scenery but also for its rich history and ghostly inhabitants. The village has a long and fascinating history, dating back to the Roman era, and it also has heavy ties to the Anglo-Saxons, but it is perhaps best known for its role in the bubonic plague outbreak of 1665.

In 1665, the bubonic plague arrived in Eyam, brought by a shipment of cloth from London. Local tailor Alexander Hadfield purchased a bundle of cloth from a merchant in London, and he kept it in his shop. His assistant, George Viccars, noticed the cloth was damp and so he opened it to help it dry out. Unbeknownst to him, the cloth was infested with plague-carrying fleas. Within weeks, both Alexander and George were dead, and before October of the same year, 20 more villagers got infected and died. The villagers made the difficult decision to quarantine themselves to prevent the disease from spreading to nearby villages. It was a brave and selfless act, and it led to the deaths of over 260 of the 800 villagers living in Eyam.

There have been many reports of paranormal activity in Eyam over the years. Many people connect this to the graves and historical sites around Eyam not being respected over the years. Some of the plague victims' gravestones were even pulled up and used as flooring for houses and barns. This could be the cause of the hauntings in this village being so widespread.

Some of the most haunted locations to find, should you want to visit the plague village, are The Miners Arms, the plague cottages, and Eyam Hall. The Miner's Arms dates back to 1630 and was originally called The Kings Arms.

It is said to house several ghosts, and people have witnessed strange sounds and footsteps, some even fleeing their beds in the middle of the night. The plague cottages are, as the name would suggest, original cottages that have survived since the plague. At least one of these cottages is said to be haunted by the ghost of a friendly-faced elderly lady in blue. She is said to wake people up at night. And Eyam Hall, one of the biggest buildings in Eyam, was built after the plague but is still said to be haunted. The ghost of a young servant woman named Sarah Mills, who drowned in the well, is often reported here.

One of the most famous ghosts is that of a young girl who died during the plague outbreak. Her ghost has been seen by many visitors, often appearing as a misty figure dressed in 17th-century clothing. Some have reported hearing her crying in the streets at night.

There have also been reports of ghostly apparitions in the many grave sites around Eyam. The ghosts are said to be the spirits of plague victims who were buried there, due to the families having to bury their own relatives during the quarantine. Visitors have reported seeing misty figures moving among the graves, and some have even heard the sound of ghostly chanting coming from the church.

Despite its sombre history, Eyam is now a picturesque village full of amazing places to visit. So why not visit the graves of those who made the ultimate sacrifice during the plague, or pop into The Miners Arms for a pint with its resident spirits? I am sure, either way, you are in for a great visit.

The Red Lion Inn - Avebury

The Red Lion Inn and the Avebury Stones

Avebury is a small village in Wiltshire, which is mostly encircled by a prehistoric monument, called the Stone Circle, or the Avebury Ring.

The Avebury Ring is a Neolithic site located in the county of Wiltshire in England. It is one of the most impressive and significant prehistoric monuments in Europe, consisting of three stone circles, two long barrows, and a large ditch and bank earthwork.

The site is estimated to be over 4,000 years old and was built during the Neolithic period, around 2,600 BC, although there is evidence of farmers using the land here 6000 years ago.

The construction of the Avebury Ring began with the building of a large bank and ditch surrounding the site, which was then followed by the construction of the stone circles. The stones used at Avebury were transported from as far away as 25 miles, and the largest stones weigh over 40 tons each.

The Avebury ring is the oldest stone ring that is known to be in existence anywhere in the world and is even older than Stonehenge, which can be found 20 miles south of Avebury.

The purpose of the site is not entirely clear, but it is believed to have had a significant religious or spiritual meaning for the people who built it. It is thought that the circles were used for rituals, such as ceremonies to celebrate the changing of the seasons or to honour their ancestors.

Over the years, the site has undergone various periods of neglect and destruction. In the 17th century, many of the stones were removed and used for building materials, and the site was even used as a livestock pen at one point. However, in the 20th century, efforts were made to preserve the site, and it was eventually designated as a UNESCO World Heritage Site. But, as with many of the other locations we have already covered, an area with such a long and unusual history seems destined to also be one of the most haunted locations in the country. One of the buildings that house many of these ghosts, is the Red Lion Inn.

The Red Lion Inn is a historic pub located in the village of Avebury, inside the famous Avebury stone circle. The building dates back to the 17th century and has served as an inn for centuries, offering a warm and welcoming atmosphere to travellers and locals alike.

One of the most famous ghosts said to haunt the Red Lion Inn is the spirit of a former landlady named Florrie. She is believed to have died at the hands of her husband when he came home from fighting in the English civil war and found her in bed with another man. Her new lover was shot dead, Florrie was stabbed to death, and her body was thrown into the well. Her spirit has been seen by many visitors and staff over the years. Her ghost is said to wander the building, often appearing in the upstairs bedrooms, and sometimes moving objects or causing other disturbances. Perhaps the strangest fact of all about Florrie, is that her remains are said to still be in the well... which is now a glass-topped table that you can request to sit at in the Red Lion Inn and spend your time there staring down into the 86 ft hole. If you are like me and would class yourself as a bearded gentleman, you are also in luck. Florrie is known to have an attraction to men with beards.

Another ghostly presence at the Red Lion Inn is that of a highwayman who is said to have been executed nearby. He is said to appear as a shadowy figure in the bar area and has been known to move objects or cause glasses to fall off shelves. The sound of hooves can also be heard as an invisible carriage pulls onto the cobbles outside the inn. Some have also claimed to see the headless horseman that goes along with one such carriage.

The sound of children laughing and running can be heard in the upstairs rooms, as well as in the cellar. Then there is the spirit of the farmer who is claimed to have owned the building before it was an Inn, who legend says was murdered. He is seen all around the building, often carrying a knife.

Even with its haunted reputation, the Red Lion Inn is still a popular destination for visitors who are interested in its history and the supernatural. Many visitors come to the inn to experience its ghostly presence firsthand, while others simply enjoy the cosy atmosphere and the traditional English pub food and drink.

Stirling Castle - Scotland

Stirling Castle, Stirling, Scotland

Stirling Castle is one of the most historically significant castles in Scotland, located in the city of Stirling. The castle sits on a rocky hilltop, overlooking the River Forth and the surrounding countryside. Its strategic location made it an important fortification and royal residence throughout Scotland's history.

The origins of the castle date back to the early Middle Ages, with the first mention of a fortification on the site in the 12th century. However, it wasn't until the 15th and 16th centuries that the castle became the grand royal palace that it is today. During this time, Stirling Castle was a favourite residence of the Scottish monarchs, including James IV and Mary, Queen of Scots.

The castle played a key role in many significant events in Scottish history, including the Wars of Scottish Independence in the 13th and 14th centuries. In 1297, William Wallace famously led a Scottish victory over the English army at the Battle of Stirling Bridge, which was fought near the castle.

In the 16th century, the castle was the site of a dramatic siege during the Scottish Reformation. Mary, Queen of Scots, was forced to surrender the castle to the Protestant rebels in 1560, marking a turning point in Scotland's religious history.

The castle underwent many changes over the centuries, including the addition of the Royal Palace in the 16th century and significant renovations in the 19th and 20th centuries. Today, visitors can explore the castle's rich history and stunning architecture, including the Great Hall, the Chapel Royal, and the King's and Queen's Apartments.

With such a long and turbulent history, it is no wonder that Stirling Castle is said to be one of the most haunted places in Scotland. Many visitors and staff members have reported strange occurrences, including unexplained noises, cold spots, and ghostly apparitions.

One of the most famous ghosts said to haunt Stirling Castle is the Green Lady. This ghostly apparition is said to be the spirit of a woman who lived in the castle during the 16th century. According to legend, the Green Lady was a servant girl who worked in the castle during the reign of Mary, Queen of Scots. She was said to be in love with a soldier who was killed in battle, and she died of a broken heart soon after.

The Green Lady is said to appear to visitors dressed in a green gown, carrying a bunch of keys. She is often seen wandering the castle's corridors and rooms and is said to be particularly active in the castle's Queen's Apartments. There have been many reported sightings of the Green Lady over the years, with visitors and staff alike reporting strange apparitions and unexplained noises. Some have even reported feeling a cold draft and the presence of an unseen entity.

One of the numerous encounters with the Green Lady occurred in the early 19th century when a soldier stationed at the castle claimed to have seen her walking through a wall. He described her as a beautiful young woman dressed in green and was so unnerved by the experience that he requested a transfer from the castle

Another intriguing ghost story associated with Stirling Castle is that of the "Highland Ghost." This ghostly apparition is said to be the spirit of a Highland soldier who was killed during a battle outside the castle walls in the 18th century. According to legend, the Highland Ghost appears as a spectral figure dressed in traditional Highland clothing, including a kilt and plaid. He is said to appear suddenly and without warning and is often seen wandering the castle's corridors and rooms.

An example of an encounter with the Highland Ghost occurred in the 1930s when two stonemasons were working on the castle's battlements. As they worked, they suddenly heard the sound of bagpipes playing a mournful tune. When they turned around, they saw the ghostly figure of the Highland soldier standing before them, playing a set of bagpipes. The apparition then vanished into thin air, leaving the stonemasons shaken and unnerved.

The third most well-known ghost at Stirling Castle is known as the Pink Lady. The exact identity of the Pink Lady seems to be up for debate, with some claiming she was a maid who died in childbirth, and others believing she is the ghost of Mary Queen of Scots herself. She's seen wearing a flowing pink gown, often walking from the castle to the nearby Church of the Holy Rood/Rude.

In addition to these well-known ghosts, there have been many other reported hauntings at Stirling Castle, including the ghost of a drummer boy, a headless woman, and even the ghost of King James IV, who died at the Battle of Flodden in 1513.

Stirling Castle remains one of Scotland's most popular tourist attractions, attracting visitors from all over the world who come to marvel at its history and soak up its unique atmosphere. For those who are brave enough, there are even ghost tours available, offering a chance to explore the castle's haunted halls and maybe even catch a glimpse of one of its resident ghosts.

Hauntings, Ghosts & Spirits - Honourable Mentions:

If the last chapters have taught us anything, it is that the UK has had a very long, troubled and sometimes gruesome history. We have also learned that locations with such a long and violent history, seem to be a hotspot for paranormal activity that comes in many forms. But we have also found evidence of houses that appear to have poltergeist activity. So perhaps this shows that a location doesn't need to have a colourful past to have a resident spirit.

There is evidence that there are more average houses with ghosts or spirits also calling them home than there are castles or mansions. This greatly adds to the possible number of haunted locations around the UK and even the world. I could have mentioned other locations that can be found on "top 10 haunted locations" lists, but as these lists seem to change every year, and as we don't truly understand the phenomena, how can we truly claim one location is more haunted than another? We also have to contend with the owners of older buildings that are struggling financially, suddenly claiming their pub/hotel/restaurant is haunted. Ghost tours and investigation teams paying to have the location to themselves overnight has become a big money earner in recent years, and so we have to remain slightly sceptical of any claims of a haunting.

That being said, I think it is also safe to assume that everyone has either seen something unexplainable or knows someone who has, which just tells us that these phenomena are very widespread and multifaceted. But if it is something that so many people have experienced, why is it still so ridiculed and not really understood?

Paranormal investigators have spent decades trying to study these experiences hoping to get a better understanding of what is truly going on. Unfortunately, without proper scientific processes, it has left many arguing over their opinions instead of working together to find the real truth. This has also led to every pub, village or hotel being given the title of 'most haunted' at some point, as there is no proper measure of how haunted a location truly is.

Our only hope seems to lie with a truly unbiased, scientific study of these phenomena. But with the topic of ghosts or poltergeists being the subject of so much disdain, this also means that anyone hoping to conduct a scientific study into the phenomena would struggle to find proper funding to help their efforts, and would then face this ridicule themselves in their career. So this means that most reputable scientists won't go near the subject.

So where do we go from here, with our aim of understanding hauntings, ghosts and spirits? In my humble opinion, I believe the investigators who are already out there, spending endless nights in these locations are still the answer to our problems. Although I also believe that they need more scientific training, so that when they do encounter something strange, they can document it properly so the data can be compared to data from other locations.

What if you believe you have something strange going on in your own home? What do *I* suggest you do? Well, again in my personal opinion, I think the first thing you need to realise is that from the data we *do* have, you have nothing to worry about. There are probably hundreds of thousands of examples of experiences, and maybe a handful of those have claims of people being physically injured, with a high percentage of *those injured* by objects being thrown. So this shows that you are definitely more likely to be experiencing a spirit that means you no harm.

So what should you do? If you're brave enough, you can investigate for yourself. Don't worry, you don't need to spend thousands on fancy technology. The best piece of equipment you can use is your own senses. But if you do want evidence that you can show to others, a few things that I'd suggest are a torch (if you are investigating at night), some kind of digital voice recorder, a digital thermometer and a camera. Turn off all other appliances, including phones, so that they are not able to interfere with any technology being used, and then collect as much data as possible.

If the idea of a spirit living in your home is too much to face on your own, there are several teams out there who will come and investigate for you. But please remember to take what they say to you with a healthy amount of scepticism.

They may have their own opinions on things like poltergeists or even demons, and you wouldn't want someone coming into your home, using this experience to help their ghost-hunting business by claiming they fought a demon in your bedroom, and then when they leave you are left frightened, unable to sleep in your own house. Any team should come into your home trying to disprove your claims of a spirit *first*, starting by ruling out things like high electromagnetic fields, usually caused by older appliances or bad wiring giving unwanted effects to those around them. Only when no other influence can be found, after a thorough search of the location, should an actual paranormal investigation start.

Do your research and find a team that you think will work best for you, and then get a second opinion. If their opinions match, without passing information to each other, then you will be closer to having the answers you are hoping for. If you are hoping they can remove a spirit from your home, unfortunately, the evidence suggests that this is not possible, and for those who have claimed to have rid a house of its spirits, this can easily be put down to the placebo effect; the witnesses believe the activity will stop and so they don't notice the activity any more. While this may help you feel better, it won't have actually done anything and your spirit may still be there.

There is however some evidence that these spirits can hear and understand you, with this being one of the main techniques used during investigations. So it may sound overly uncomplicated, but you could try just simply asking the spirit to either leave, or at least stop interacting with yourself or the location as it is causing members of the household to be frightened. Hopefully, some of this has helped if you are experiencing something strange in your own home.

UFOs & Alien Sightings

If you say the words UFO or aliens, most people will think of Roswell, New Mexico, or Area 51. These locations are synonymous with extraterrestrial encounters, thanks to a plethora of books, movies, and TV shows that have cemented their place in popular culture. However, it is important to note that the United States is not the only country with a history of strange occurrences in the sky. In fact, the United Kingdom has a rich history of UFO sightings and encounters with extraterrestrial beings that span centuries.

One of the earliest recorded UFO sightings in the UK dates back to the 12th century when a monk reported seeing a silver object fly across the sky. Over the centuries, there have been numerous sightings of strange lights and objects in the sky, many of which have been reported by credible witnesses, including police officers and military personnel.

One of the most well-known cases in the UK is the Rendlesham Forest incident, which took place in December 1980. It involved the sighting of strange lights in the forest by US Air Force personnel stationed at the nearby RAF Woodbridge base. Some witnesses reported seeing a craft with flashing lights and landing marks on the ground. The incident has been extensively studied and debated, with some sceptics suggesting that it was a simple case of misidentification, while others maintain that it was an extraterrestrial encounter.

The Rendlesham Forest incident has become known as "Britain's Roswell," and it continues to capture the imagination of UFO enthusiasts and researchers alike. In fact, the incident has been the subject of numerous books, documentaries, and even a feature film.

Another famous incident occurred in 1995 in the town of Warminster. Residents reported hearing strange noises and seeing unusual objects in the sky. The phenomenon became so widespread that it attracted the attention of the media and sparked a wave of interest in the topic of UFOs. Some theories suggest that the strange occurrences were caused by secret military testing, while others maintain that it was a genuine encounter with an alien spacecraft.

Despite the ongoing debate and speculation surrounding these incidents, one thing is certain: they have captured the imagination of the public and continue to fascinate researchers and enthusiasts alike. Whether these sightings are the result of misidentification, secret military testing, or genuine encounters with alien spacecraft, the stories of these sightings and abductions have left an indelible mark on the cultural consciousness of the UK and the world.

The UK is home to a number of organisations and groups that study and investigate UFO sightings, including the British UFO Research Association (BUFORA) and the Association for the Scientific Study of Anomalous Phenomena (ASSAP). There are also many smaller, local groups such as my local group, BUFOG (Birmingham UFO group). These organisations have collected thousands of reports from witnesses over the years, and they continue to work towards uncovering the truth behind these mysterious sightings.

One of the most intriguing aspects of the UK's UFO history is the sheer variety of sightings and encounters. Some reports describe seeing strange lights in the sky, while others detail encounters with alien beings. Some witnesses report feeling a sense of fear or unease during their encounters, while others describe a feeling of awe and wonder.

One particularly strange case occurred in 1974 when a man named Zigmund Adamski disappeared from his home in West Yorkshire. His body was later found on top of a coal heap, with strange burns and marks on his body. Some UFO enthusiasts speculate that Adamski was abducted by aliens and then returned to Earth, while others suggest that his death was the result of a government cover-up.

Another famous UFO sighting in the UK occurred in 1977 in the town of Broad Haven, Wales. A group of schoolchildren reported seeing a silver flying saucer land in a field near their school and even claimed to have seen an alien figure emerge from the craft. The incident was widely reported in the media and sparked a wave of interest in the topic of UFOs across the UK.

In the years since, numerous other sightings and encounters have been reported across the UK. In 2008, a UFO sighting in the town of Morpeth in Northumberland made national headlines, with numerous witnesses claiming to have seen a silver disc-shaped object hovering in the sky for several minutes before disappearing. In 2016, a man in

Nottinghamshire reported seeing a UFO hovering above his house for several minutes before flying off at incredible speed.

Despite the ongoing debate over the legitimacy of these sightings and encounters, there is no doubt that they have captured the imagination of the public and continue to fascinate researchers and enthusiasts alike. For many, the question of whether or not we are alone in the universe remains one of the greatest mysteries of our time, and the evidence provided by these sightings and encounters only adds to the intrigue.

As technology continues to advance and our understanding of the universe expands, it is possible that we may one day find definitive proof of extraterrestrial life. Until then, the stories and sightings of UFOs and aliens in the UK and around the world will continue to captivate our imaginations and fuel our curiosity.

The Warminster 'Thing'

A newspaper headline about the Warminster 'Thing' 1965

Warminster, a small market town in Wiltshire, is usually a very quiet, peaceful place to visit. But during the last few weeks of 1964, into 1965 and beyond, this was set to change.

This story starts in the early morning of Christmas day 1964 when some residents were awoken by strange sounds. Some described it as starting with something that sounded like twigs hitting a roof and then more like giant hailstones. But the sound soon escalated into a strange humming sound that eventually faded away to a distant whisper.

Later that morning, a local woman by the name of Mrs Marjorie Bye was on her way to the Holy

Communion Service at Christ Church. She first noticed a "crackling sound" coming from the nearby Bell Hill area of the town. As she approached, she then described what happened to her next as a "sonic attack". Mrs Bye felt as though she was being pushed down by an invisible force, hearing a very loud noise and feeling the vibrations pushing on her head, neck and shoulders like "invisible fingers of sound".

She contacted the local newspaper, The Warminster Journal, and told them of her experiences. They published an article a few weeks later, written by journalist Arthur Shuttlewood. This was soon followed by around thirty other witnesses from in and around Warminster contacting the newspaper with their own events. Many of them heard something very similar. Warminster's postmaster, Roger Rump, along with around 30 British Army troops stationed at Knook Camp, were among those who contacted the newspaper. They told similar stories of noises of "roof tiles being lifted and slammed back down again" followed by a high-pitched whining or humming sound.

Even though there were so many witnesses to this strange sound, there was no explanation offered.

Within six months, the accounts of strange noises started to be accompanied by sightings of peculiar objects in the sky. A silent cigar-shaped object covered in winking lights was seen in both May and June 1965 by multiple witnesses. Some of these unidentified objects were seen to hover around the skies of Warminster for up to thirty minutes, eventually slowly drifting away silently. Weird lights in the sky were also witnessed by many locals, which were described as being like "huge eyes in the sky".

The journalist at the Warminster Journal, Arthur Shuttlewood, who had published the first article on the 'thing' had begun to collect all of these statements from witnesses, although he remained very sceptical of the whole thing. This was until September 28th 1965, when he had his own sighting. Witnessed from the window of his own home, Shuttlewood claimed to have seen a huge cigar-shaped object gliding through the sky. He reached for his camera and pointed it towards the object, hoping to capture evidence of the sighting. Unfortunately, when he tried to have the film developed, he found it had been burned and was unsalvageable. He also claimed that during his sighting, his wristwatch stopped working and that he felt pins and needles in his hand and arm.

A few weeks prior to Shuttlewood's sighting, a local factory worker named Gordon Faulkner, succeeded in capturing one of these objects on film. He gave this photo to, then still sceptical, Arthur Shuttlewood who passed it to the British national tabloid newspaper, The Daily Mirror. It was published on September 10th 1965, alongside an article written by Shuttlewood that was entitled:

"THE THING: a strange story of the goings-on in the skies above a country town."

This article not only brought a lot of publicity to the small town of Warminster but also thousands of people, from all over the world, flocked to the area hoping to experience the 'thing' for themselves. On some days, there were an estimated eight thousand more people in the town.

Before all of this newly found fame had caused thousands to rush into Warminster, the locals were already worried about the occurrences, and so a town meeting was called on Friday, August 27, 1965. This meeting went on for an hour, with members of the national press in attendance, as locals took turns explaining what they had seen or heard and asking officials what they were planning to do about their fears, which ranged from worrying about damage to property to fears that the 'thing' was a danger to Earth.

This meeting also had its own strange moment, which some sci-fi fans will appreciate more than the locals did at the time. The Town Council Chair was handed a telegram during the meeting, that read:

"Investigations completed. Invasion fears are unfounded — Dr Who."

In the months and even years following, Warminster locals continued to hear the noises and had more and more sightings of craft in the sky. There were even multiple witnesses who claimed to see another craft, accompanied by the strange sounds, on the one-year

234

anniversary of the original occurrence, on Christmas Day.

Warminster had very quickly earned itself the reputation of being a UFO hotspot. There are reports and anecdotal statements of hundreds of sightings during the years of the 'thing' and more and more investigators, both amateur and professional, were still flocking to the area. The BBC even came to the area to film a documentary on the phenomenon, called "Pie In The Sky". The journalist, Arthur Shuttlewood, continued to collect any and all data on the phenomena and has written three books on the subject.

Eventually, over the years, the number of sightings dwindled and all but came to an end. The number of people travelling to Warminster also slowed down, and in recent years it is much closer to the original peaceful market town that it was before any of these goings-on occurred. You *can* still see evidence of the UFO craze in the town, as some local shops still offer UFO-themed memorabilia and toys.

So what *was* going on in Warminster in the 1960s? Were the residents being stalked by real extraterrestrial craft, which were causing strange vibrations and sounds in the air? Or was it something much more mundane, such as mass hysteria or misidentification of a more natural phenomenon?

There have been strange sounds heard in the sky for decades, all around the world. They have been dubbed "sky trumpets" and there are videos of them all over social media of people recording as they wonder what is going on. These sounds have left experts dumbfounded and unable to explain what is causing them, with scientists only able to offer guesses for what *could* be responsible for them. Theories range from tectonic plates grinding together, atmospheric pressure, telephone transmissions and top-secret military aircraft. Obviously, with strange things in the skies, people have claimed that there could be a link with UFOs. But if Warminster is anything to go by, they may not be far from the truth. NASA also gave their opinion on these sky trumpets, and claimed that it could just be Earth's "background noise".

Perhaps if and when we find an answer for these sounds currently plaguing people around the world, we may have a better understanding of what the 'thing' in Warminster was.

The Calvine UFO photo

The Calvine UFO photo: Left; A recreation of the photo based on its description, Right; The leaked original

The Calvine UFO photo, considered by some ufologists to be a major piece of evidence for the existence of UFOs, has been the subject of debate for decades. The photo, taken in 1990 in Perthshire, reportedly shows a diamond-shaped craft that was approximately 100 feet in diameter. Two hikers claimed to have taken six photos of the craft and watched it for 10 minutes before it disappeared at high speed when RAF jets approached it. The photos were later given to Scotland's Daily Record, but when the journalist contacted the Ministry of Defence for comment, the photos and negatives were classified and locked away. Former MOD employee Nick Pope claimed that a blown-up, colour version of the photo was once displayed in his office, but it vanished due to infighting over the reality of UFOs. However, some researchers have questioned Pope's credibility and the validity of his evidence.

In 2021, when the photos were due to be released, they were classified again until 2076 due to "privacy concerns." But in 2022, journalist Dr David Clarke released one of the original photos, claiming that he found it through the former RAF press officer Craig Lindsay, who had kept a copy of the photo in his role as the press officer for the MoD in 1990. This photo has since been debated by ufologists and sceptics, with some suggesting it shows a top-secret military craft.

Despite the limited information available, the release of the original photo by Dr David Clarke provided a new avenue for debate and discussion within the UFO community. While many ufologists hoped to prove its validity, sceptics argued that the photo merely showed a rock and its reflection in some water.

Other theories have been put forth as well, including the possibility that the photo depicts a top-secret military craft. However, the lack of visible wings or means of propulsion makes it difficult to determine the object's nature. Additionally, the object's large size would require a significant advance in technology to remain airborne.

Regardless of the photo's contents, the fact that the photos were classified for so long has led many to believe that there must be something of interest in them. The possibility of a cover-up by the government only adds to the mystery surrounding the Calvine UFO case.

Though the release of the original photo provided some insight into the case, the majority of the photos remain classified until 2076. The search for the original witnesses, including Kevin Russell, continues to this day. While the release of the photo has sparked renewed interest in the case, it is unclear whether the truth about the Calvine UFO will ever be fully revealed.

So does this photo show a UFO in the skies above Perthshire? Is it the best UFO photo ever taken? Is it an original, or has it been tampered with? These are all questions the UFO community would love to have answered. Luckily, the Daily Record newspaper has come forward with the name of the witness, Kevin

Russell, and information such as that he was working as a hotel porter at the time the photos were taken. Kevin would now be in his 50s (at the time of writing).

UFO investigators have searched directories etc for anyone with that name, hoping to find the one person who will have the answers to all of their questions, contacting 150 Kevin Russells, but none of them confirmed it was him they were looking for. So unfortunately, even though we now seemingly have one of the original photos, we still aren't much closer to finding out what was really seen that fateful day in 1990 in the skies above Calvine.

The Rendlesham Forest Incident (RFI)

Replica of the UFO at the landing site - Rendlesham Forest

Dubbed "Britain's Roswell", The Rendlesham Forest incident is one of the most well-known UFO events in the UK. Unfortunately, the incident has become a battleground for sceptics and UFO enthusiasts alike, filled with politics, backstabbing and infighting. However, despite contradicting accounts, I will attempt to present the agreed-upon information by the majority of researchers. This means, unfortunately, there may be a lot of information missing from this chapter. I would highly recommend researching this for yourself if you are interested in knowing more.

So, for this case, we have to go back to 1980.

The incident began on December 26, 1980, when three US Air Force security patrolmen stationed at the nearby RAF Woodbridge military base reported seeing a strange object in the sky. The object was described as being "triangular in shape, with coloured lights and a metallic appearance." Initially, the patrolmen thought it was a downed aircraft, but upon closer inspection, they realised it was something completely unknown.

On the night of December 27, 1980, Halt was at an officer's dinner, when Lt Bruce Englund told him "the UFO is back". Halt and his team ventured into the forest to investigate the strange lights. They reported seeing a glowing object moving through the trees, which they described as being "metallic in appearance." The object seemed to be emitting a strange mist or fog, and the team reported feeling a "static" or "electricity" in the air.

As they approached the object, it suddenly disappeared. Later that night, the object reappeared, and Halt recorded his observations on his tape recorder, which captured their observations and experiences during the incident. The recording is commonly known as the "Halt Tape" and has become a significant piece of evidence in the Rendlesham Forest UFO incident.

On the Halt Tape, Halt and his team can be heard reporting their observations of strange lights and objects in the sky. Halt describes seeing a "strange, eerie" light moving through the trees, which he describes as "like an eye winking at you." He also reports feeling "static" or "electricity" in the air and describes the presence of a "bright white light" in the sky.

Throughout the recording, Halt and his team express confusion and disbelief at what they are seeing. They describe the lights as "bizarre," "weird," and "unbelievable." At one point, Halt remarks that the object they are observing is "definitely a UFO."

The Halt Tape also captures the sounds of the forest at night, including animal noises and rustling trees. At certain points in the recording, a strange beeping noise can be heard in the background, which some have suggested is evidence of communication between the UFO and a ground-based transmitter.

Over the next few days, several other witnesses came forward, reporting seeing strange lights and objects in the sky. The incident was officially investigated by both the UK and US governments, but no conclusive explanation was ever given. Some officials dismissed the sightings as misidentified natural phenomena or military exercises, while others suggested that the objects were of extraterrestrial origin. Most sceptics put the sighting down to a combination of the Orfordness Lighthouse in the distance and a small meteor falling to the ground inside the forest.

In recent years, there have been several attempts to revisit and re-examine the Rendlesham Forest incident. In 2019, the UK's Ministry of Defence released previously classified documents related to the incident, shedding new light on the government's handling of the incident.

Despite the release of these documents, the Rendlesham Forest UFO incident remains a topic of fascination and debate among UFO enthusiasts and sceptics alike. And despite the 40th anniversary of the RFI having just passed, there are still differing versions of events between witnesses, and those who try to claim that they were present but cannot be verified.

Are they just trying to put their name into one of the biggest UFO cases in the world, perhaps for the fame that seems to follow those involved? Who knows. But maybe one day we will have the full truth surrounding this incident. Until then, we will just have to try to find the nuggets of truth in the sea of disinformation. There are researchers out there trying to piece together the real version of events. People like Gary Heseltine, an ex-UK policeman turned UFO investigator, who has released a book filled with years of his research, entitled "Non-Human". In my opinion, this book appears to be the closest yet to the real events of the RFI and the truth about those who were there to witness it. If you want to know more, I would highly recommend starting there.

The Sheffield Triangles

The Peak District, Sheffield

On the 24th March 1997, the police in Sheffield received numerous calls of a low-flying aircraft that had been seen flying over mountains and was then feared to have crashed, after a bright flash was seen and a loud explosion heard.

The police then began a huge search of the area, even alerting the local hospitals of a potential plane going down and that there may be casualties or survivors needing assistance. They then contacted Air Traffic Control and the RAF and were told by both that no planes were missing and that there were no military planes in the area at the time of the alleged crash.

The following morning, the police set up an emergency phone line for any other members of the public with information to contact them. They received a considerable amount of calls, with people claiming to have witnessed a low-flying plane, followed by military jets, and hearing the subsequent explosion. With so many witnesses to the incident, police decided to scale up the search area, called in more mountain rescue volunteers and sent out more helicopters. Hoping to find the wreckage of this aircraft, the RAF also called in to help with the search, which implemented a ten-mile exclusion zone around Howden reservoir.

By 2 pm, still nothing had been found and so the police decided to call off the search. Still confused by the lack of evidence of a crash, and with so many people claiming to have seen and heard a plane go down, other possible explanations were discussed, including small planes performing a drug drop and some even considering the possibility of a sighting of the 'ghost plane' thought to haunt the Peak District. The police were never able to discover what had happened that night, and said later that they "remain open-minded about what was behind the sightings".

What makes this case so interesting is that a large number of the witnesses who claim to have seen the low-flying aircraft, also claiming it wasn't your average plane, describing it as a 'large black triangle'. Many of the accounts claimed to have seen the triangle moving slowly and silently across the sky, and moving off quickly when "at least six Tornado jets" started to pursue it. It then vanished behind a mountain, and soon after the explosion was heard.

The MOD was asked to give information on this incident by the UK Parliament a year later, and they claimed that a low-flying military air exercise was taking place in the area on 24th March 1997, although the RAF then disagreed with these claims, saying they had no aircraft in that area and that no such exercise took place.

A seismologist at Edinburgh's seismology department then added to the story, confirming that two sonic booms were heard on the 24th March at 21:52 and 22:06, adding that the likely explanations were either an aircraft travelling at supersonic speeds or space debris falling to earth. The RAF then also denied the claims that any of their craft travelled faster than the speed of sound, reiterating that it is illegal to break the sound barrier over land in the UK and that they had no record of any sonic booms on that night.

The fact that the MOD (Ministry of Defence) was saying one thing, and the RAF another, was enough to spark talks of a cover-up. But what were they covering up? Perhaps the RAF had been performing a classified test of some sort of aircraft the public was not allowed to know about, and so publicly, they had to deny it. But surely the MOD would also know this, and would not have confirmed an exercise took place. And if a new type of jet was being tested, and broke the sound barrier illegally, this also would explain why the RAF were so quick to say it was not them.

But this explanation still leaves us with the question of what did all those witnesses see, who claimed to have seen a large black triangle in the sky? And why was it followed or pursued by "at least 6 tornado jets"? Did the RAF detect something strange on their radar, and intercept it in the skies over the Peak District, and was there a possible collision, or something being shot down? Is this why the RAF set up the ten-mile exclusion zone around the reservoir? Were they there attempting to retrieve the wreckage of either their own jet or the strange triangular craft? It seems there are still several unanswered questions, whether you are on the UFO believer or more sceptical side of this incident. Such as why were the RAF breaking the sound barrier in the skies above the city of Sheffield?

Broad Haven School

Broad Haven pupils with their drawings of what they saw

This case is probably one of my favourite UK sightings. It has everything a UFO investigator would want from a sighting. Multiple witness testimonies all corroborating each other, a landed craft, a sighting of actual creatures and evidence of an investigation by MoD officials.

Broad Haven is a small, quiet village and seaside town in Pembrokeshire, Wales. But starting in February 1977, this quiet was disrupted by a number of UFO sightings in the area, which went on to be dubbed the 'Broad Haven Triangle'. The children of Broad Haven Primary School were outside playing during their morning break, when a number of them

251

saw a silver, cigar-shaped object hovering in the sky above the school's playing fields.

According to the children's accounts, the object had a domed shape in its middle third and emitted a low humming sound. The children watched as the object descended and landed in a nearby field, before quickly taking off again and disappearing into the distance. Some of the children also claimed to have seen a humanoid figure dressed in a silver suit exiting the craft once it had landed.

The children reported what they had seen to the school's headmaster, Ralph Llewellyn, who initially dismissed it as a prank or a figment of the children's imaginations. However, when more sightings began to be reported in the surrounding area, Llewellyn began to take the incident more seriously. He then had the children draw what they had seen, and he was then convinced after seeing their drawing all showing the same or very similar objects.

This UFO sighting was not an isolated incident. In the weeks and months that followed, a number of other sightings were reported in the same area, leading some to speculate that a "Broad Haven Triangle" existed, similar to the

Bermuda Triangle. One of the most notable of these sightings occurred just a few weeks after the Broad Haven Primary School incident, when a local hotel owner reported seeing an object land in a field next to her hotel. The object was described as an 'upside down saucer' and two faceless humanoid creatures with pointed heads, and was said to have remained in the field for several minutes before taking off again. Other sightings included reports of strange lights in the sky, unexplained aircraft flying low over the countryside, and strange objects landing in fields and on beaches.

The Broad Haven UFO sightings attracted national media attention, and soon a team of investigators arrived in the town to try to get to the bottom of the mystery.

These investigators spent several weeks interviewing witnesses and gathering evidence. Many of their investigations led them to conclude that the sightings were most likely the result of a combination of misidentification of natural phenomena and hoaxes. However, many of the witnesses remained convinced that they had seen something genuinely unexplainable, and their stories remain unchanged now, more than 40 years later.

The Broad Haven Primary School UFO sighting and the other incidents in the surrounding area remain some of the most fascinating and mysterious cases in the history of UFO sightings.

While sceptics may dismiss the sightings as the result of misidentification or hoaxes, the fact that so many people in the area reported seeing similar objects and phenomena suggests that something truly unusual was happening.

These sightings also had a profound impact on the town and its residents. Many of the witnesses were children at the time of the incident, and the experience stayed with them for the rest of their lives.

In recent years, interest in the Broad Haven UFO incident has seen a resurgence, with new witnesses coming forward and new theories being proposed. While the truth of what happened that day may never be known, the legacy of the Broad Haven UFO sighting continues to captivate and intrigue UFO enthusiasts and sceptics alike.

Berwyn Mountain Incident

The view from the summit of Cadair Berwyn

In the evening of 23rd January 1974, the inhabitants of Llandrillo and neighbouring villages around the Berwyn Mountains were startled by an event that was likened to an explosion by many eyewitnesses. According to reports, some people also witnessed lights in the sky that appeared to be falling rapidly to the ground, leaving behind a trail of fire and smoke. The occurrence soon gained notoriety as a UFO crash and was referred to as the 'Welsh Roswell.'

Police received numerous reports of strange lights in the sky and an explosion so loud it shook houses. The RAF scrambled a search and rescue team to locate the downed plane, but found nothing. Rumours of a UFO crash started swirling around communities surrounding the Berwyn mountains and once sightings started pouring in from further afield in the UK, this only added to the drama.

Eventually the Institute of Geological Sciences discovered that there had been a 3.5 magnitude earthquake at 8:38 pm on the night of the sighting. So this, added to the lack of evidence of a crash site or debris, was assumed to be the explanation for the "explosion" and the witnesses who claimed their houses shook. But what about the strange lights in the sky?

Coincidentally, there were reports of a green fireball meteor spotted in the sky around the UK, at around the same time as the earthquake, which eventually broke up around 35 km above Manchester. Those officially investigating this event found that the earthquake and fireball combined were an adequate explanation. But those who believe they saw a UFO in the skies that night, were not happy with this answer to their questions. They came to the conclusion that something must have crashed in the mountains and that the RAF and MOD covered it up. They even went as far as to conclude where they thought the crashed craft was taken. Rudloe Manor. This manor house, now known as RAF Rudloe Manor, is situated in Bath and was taken over along with many other manor houses by the MOD during WWII to be used as an ammunition dump.

After WWII ended, the other houses were given back, but Rudloe Manor was never released by the MOD and has been used ever since. This manor house just so happens to sit on top of 2,250,000 square feet of tunnels and caverns, created during Bath stone mining. Conspiracy theorists believe this is why the MOD refused to hand back the locating, and used it as 'Britain's Area 51', housing crashed UFOs, alien artefacts and perhaps even the bodies of alien beings. There have been claims of crashed UFOs in the area surrounding Rudloe Manor going all the way back to the 1940s and the History Channel TV show Ancient Aliens has covered the manor on several episodes.

Not long after the supposed alien craft crashed near Rudloe Manor in the 1940s, American journalist, Dorothy Kilgallon, wrote a newspaper article on the incident and claimed to have been given a tip-off by a high-ranking

British military official. Kilgallen investigated this, along with other high-profile cases until her suspicious death.

Dorothy Kilgallen was one of the most well-known and prominent reporters in American history. Her tenacious personality and intense columns examined major stories of her time, including the murder trial of Dr. Sam Sheppard and the Cuban Missile Crisis.

After the assassination of President, and her close friend, John F Kennedy in November of 1963, Dorothy dedicated her work to uncovering what she believed to have been a massive conspiracy and cover-up. She had a contact in the Warren Commission who leaked information to her, which she in turn published. The FBI began keeping a file on her, and tapping her phone after Dorothy refused to reveal her sources. Dorothy became the only journalist to get a private, one on one interview with Jack Ruby, the man who shot and killed Lee Harvey Oswald (the man who was charged with Kennedy's assassination). Oswald always denied being responsible and claimed he was a 'patsy' being used to cover up the truth.

In the days and weeks leading up to her death, Dorothy told friends she was going to break the case open and she had plans to travel to New Orleans to meet with an informant. Sadly, Dorothy would be found dead in her home just days before this trip, with her body found fully dressed sitting upright in her bed.

Later reports indicated that she and her friends were on the verge of locating JFK's killer. Kilgallon had just returned from an interview in Dallas, Texas when she was found, and what information she had gathered would never be revealed as her research files on both the death of JFK and Rudloe Manor were never found. The official ruling in Dorothy's death was that she died from an accidental overdose, a lethal combination of alcohol and sleeping pills. While this was the official story, many believe that Dorothy was murdered to halt her investigation into both JFKs assassination and what truly lies in the tunnels beneath Rudloe Manor.

Robert Taylor/Dechmont woods Incident

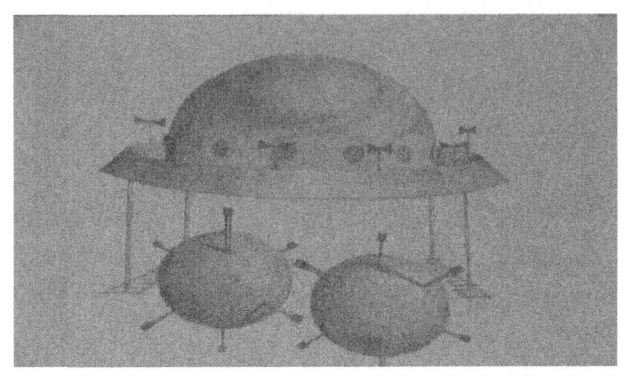

An artist's interpretation of what Robert Taylor described

The encounter Robert 'Bob' Taylor experienced on November 9th 1979 has become one of the most famous examples of a close encounter in the world, and even has the reputation as the only alien sightings that then became part of a criminal investigation.

Robert Taylor was employed by Livingston Development Corporation as a forester in the development of Livingston New Town. One day, he parked his pickup truck near the M8 motorway and took a walk with his dog up a newly-planted forestry area north of Dechmont Law. While walking down a forest track, he stumbled upon a large, metallic, circular sphere that measured 20 feet across. As he approached it, two smaller spheres dropped from the main sphere and started rolling towards him. His dog began barking and the smaller spheres latched onto his legs, dragging him towards the larger sphere. During this, Taylor heard a hissing sound and smelled an acrid odour before losing consciousness.

When he woke up 20 minutes later, the strange objects had disappeared, and Taylor was left with a deep ache in his legs and unable to talk. He crawled back to his pickup truck, which would not start, and he then walked a mile to his house to tell his wife he had been attacked by a "spaceship thing."

The police initially suspected that Taylor had been assaulted by someone unknown, but upon careful investigation, they found two ladder indentations on the ground where the craft had allegedly stood and forty small, circular holes that followed the path of the mine-like objects. There were no other tracks leading in or out of the clearing, and none of the corporation-owned vehicles had dimensions that matched the tracks. Taylor's clothes were sent for forensic analysis, which revealed a "sharp upward pull."

Despite attempts by theorists to explain the incident through other means, such as an epileptic seizure induced by a mirage from Venus, Taylor remained consistent in his story until his death in 2007 at the age of 88. He was a highly respected member of the local community, known for his honesty, and did not seek fame or significant publicity.

Personally, I have always been intrigued by Robert Taylor's story, and I think the explanation of the seizure caused by Venus is a rather ridiculous idea, even for an overly sceptical person. What *did* happen though, I cannot be sure. What Robert described is a very unique sighting, and there are also not too many sightings with so much physical evidence, with all of the marks left on Taylor's body and the clearing itself. For me, this is one of the most likely to be proven as a real UFO experience.

Clapham Wood

Clapham Wood - West Sussex

This area of Clapham, West Sussex has earned itself the reputation for being one of the creepiest places in Britain. From ghost sightings, paranormal activity and bodies being found to rumours of satanic rituals and UFO sightings, there are plenty of reasons for locals to be weary of these woods.

From 1972 to 1981, four missing people were found dead in the woods. In June 1972, Police Constable Peter Goldsmith's body was found six months after he disappeared. Three years later, a couple searching for their lost horse discovered missing pensioner Leon Foster's body. Around three years after he was first reported missing, the body of Reverend Harry Neil Snelling was found in 1978. In November 1981, Jillian Matthews, a homeless person with schizophrenia, was brutally murdered and left in the woods.

Additionally, dogs that were walking with their owners also vanished without a trace, despite extensive searches to find them. The woods were also believed to be a site for Satanic cult activity, known as the 'Friends of Hectate.' Some speculate that the stories of walkers being pulled by an unknown force and experiencing sudden feelings of sickness, shortness of breath, and overwhelming pain may be related to the devil worship practices that took place.

There were also several claims of UFO sightings, predominantly in the 1960s, with claims of strange lights in the sky and in the woodland itself. But sightings of unidentified objects in the skies over Clapham wood date back even further. During the 1700s, an elderly woman witnessed a peculiar occurrence where a bright, circular shape resembling the full moon descended into the woods, and vanished in the bushes. Following this, the woods were filled with fumes that smelled like burning matter. Unfortunately, the woman was afflicted with palsy after this encounter, causing the locals to avoid her.

Since then, reports of UFO sightings and possible landings have continued. Although many have been reported to the police and investigators, there may be numerous unreported sightings due to fear of being ridiculed.

In 1968, an insomniac spotted a saucer-shaped object hovering over the nearby woods through his kitchen window at 2 am. He immediately notified the police, but upon their arrival, the UFO had already vanished.

Similarly, in October 1972, while driving home alone along Findon Road, a telephone engineer witnessed a large saucer-shaped object in the sky, which made a circle of the area before abruptly zooming away. Another sighting came from a couple walking near Long Furlong, West Sussex, who mistook an object in the western sky for Venus, until it began to move rapidly north. When it was over Clapham Wood, a beam of light descended vertically from it and then quickly retracted before darting away to the North-East.

There are not as many sightings of strange experiences in recent years, and sceptics will explain away the more historical sightings as rumours and stories told by those with active imaginations. Whatever the case may be surrounding the paranormal encounters, there is no denying that something peculiar has been happening there, with so many bodies and animals disappearing in these woods. Is this due to aliens or spirits? Or satanic rituals? It is hard to say without hard evidence. But one thing is for certain, I won't be wandering into Clapham woods alone any time soon, especially at night.

Bonnybridge Sightings - Falkirk Triangle

The Sunken Gardens - Bonnybridge

Bonnybridge, a small town nestled in the Scottish Lowlands, may not be the first place that comes to mind when you think of UFO sightings. Yet, this sleepy town has earned itself a global reputation as the "UFO capital of the world," with almost 300 sightings reported annually over the last three decades. The question is: why? What makes this little town such a hotspot for unidentified flying objects?

One of the most famous sightings happened in 1992 when local businessman James Walker was driving between Falkirk and Bonnybridge. He was forced to stop his car on a deserted country road when a bright, star-shaped object blocked his way, hovering above the road. The object then zoomed off at a tremendous speed, leaving Walker understandably shaken. Since then, a plethora of residents and UFO enthusiasts have come forward to share their own encounters with strange flying objects, with a study indicating that most Bonnybridge residents have seen a UFO at some point in their lives.

Reports range from strange hovering lights and cigar-shaped flying objects to UFOs that buzz loudly over vehicles, causing great alarm to motorists. Some have even claimed to have been kidnapped by alien entities in the Falkirk Triangle before being whisked away onto flying saucers for further examination. The region has the highest number of UFO sightings in the UK and possibly even the world. The question remains, what is it about the Scottish Lowlands that makes it so attractive to UFOs?

One theory is that the Falkirk Triangle, which encompasses Bonnybridge, is a window into another dimension. Some suggest that the thinning between worlds is more fragile around Bonnybridge than elsewhere in the UK, making it an ideal slipping point between dimensional realms. Others believe that, like the Forth & Clyde Canal, an intergalactic stream or highway runs through the Falkirk Triangle, leading to a celestial stopover in the Scottish Lowlands.

Paranormal expert, Malcolm Robinson, along with local councillor Billy Buchanan, have appealed to four British Prime Ministers – David Cameron, Tony Blair, Gordon Brown, and John Major – to launch an urgent probe into what is happening in the skies above the town. Malcolm has investigated strange phenomena for over forty years, including many of the cases I have mentioned, and has written several brilliant books on the topics. From UFO sightings to poltergeists, there is nothing Malcolm won't research and investigate to help us all get to the bottom of what is really going on in the paranormal world.

Some would argue that the unexplained flying objects may be of terrestrial origin, possibly related to secret military training. With its remote location and rolling landscape, the Scottish Lowlands are an ideal flight-testing area.

While the Scottish Highlands have their fair share of unexplained phenomena, from ghost lights to Will-o'-the-wisps, these are often explained away as gases emanating from the boggy terrain. Such gases produce balls of light that can be seen dancing over the moors, accounting for some of the smaller sightings. However, this explanation fails to account for the larger, more intense experiences that have been reported in Bonnybridge and the Falkirk Triangle.

So, are Bonnybridge and the Falkirk Triangle special locations? What is really happening there? Hopefully, one day, we may finally get an answer. The mystery surrounding the town and its otherworldly visitors continues to fascinate and intrigue UFO enthusiasts and sceptics alike.

West Freugh Incident

Aerial view of RAF West Freugh - now known as MoD West Freugh

In 1937, RAF West Freugh was established as a training ground for armament operations. Over time, it grew to include facilities for training navigators, observers, and bomb aimers during the Second World War. However, its most notable moment in history occurred in April 1957, when radar at the Ministry of Supply Bombing Trials Unit, which was headquartered at RAF West Freugh, witnessed something very strange indeed.

During a test bombing exercise monitored by radar units, civilian operators were instructed to switch off their sets due to a delay. However, one unit at Balscalloch near Corsewall Point failed to receive the message and observed an unidentified echo, which was large and solid, hovering above the Irish Sea for 10 minutes at an initial altitude of 50,000 feet (15,000 m). The object was almost stationary and located about 20 to 25 miles (40 km) north of Stranraer. The echo's altitude then increased to 70,000 feet (21,000 m).

The Balscalloch Unit then contacted West Freugh air traffic control and informed the controller that there were multiple moving targets. These targets were moving at thousands of miles per hour, and their echoes were unlike anything the radar operator had seen before. West Freugh and Ardwell Unit, located 14 miles to their south, both observed the targets and confirmed the sighting. The position began to move northeast at speeds gradually increasing up to 70 mph (110 km/h) and at a height of 54,000 feet (16,000 m) after ten minutes.

Another radar station, now switched back on, confirmed the target and noted that after the radar echo had travelled around 20 miles (32 km), it performed an "impossible" sharp turn and proceeded in a south-easterly direction while increasing its speed. The third station then tracked four objects at 14,000 feet (4,300 m) which was also confirmed by Balscalloch. The echoes were significantly larger than those of regular planes and were closer in size to that of a ship.

Following the incident, RAF intelligence ordered all radar stations in the UK to be on a 24-hour alert. A few days later, the civilian operators informed various newspapers, including the Sunday Dispatch, about the incident, which was then published on 7 April 1957. An Air Ministry spokesman declined to make a detailed statement until a full report had been reviewed by experts, while Wing Commander Walter Whitworth, who was the Commanding Officer of RAF West Freugh, issued an Air Ministry-approved statement.

"I have been ordered by the Air Ministry to say nothing about the object. I am not allowed to reveal its position, course and speed. From the moment of picking it up, it was well within our area. It was an object of some substance - quite definitely not a freak. No mistake could have been made by the civilians operating the sets. They are fully qualified and experienced officers."

Parliamentary inquiries were made regarding the incident, and the Air Ministry was compelled to acknowledge their inability to provide an explanation. Due to the incident's disclosure to the media, the RAF kept meticulous internal records, although the specifics of official records are safeguarded under the Official Secrets Act. However, in a document containing minutes from an RAF meeting in 1970, Whitworth further remarked that:

"After remaining stationary for a short time, the UFO began to rise vertically with no forward movement, rising rapidly to approximately 60,000 feet (18,000 m) in much less than a minute. The UFO then began to move in an easterly direction, slowly at first but later accelerating very fast and travelling towards Newton Stewart, losing height on the way. Suddenly the UFO turned to the southeast, picking up speed to 240 mph (390 km/h) as it moved towards the Isle of Man. It was at this stage that the radar signals became contradictory. Balscalloch tracked a single 'object' at high altitude while Ardwell picked up what appeared to be four separate objects moving behind each other at a height of 14,000 feet (4,300 m). As the echoes disappeared; all three radars fleetingly traced the four smaller UFOs 'trailing' behind the larger object. The UFO had been tracked for 36 minutes."

With such detailed quotes from radar operators, who were all highly trained to track aircraft, showing that they had no idea what they were looking at, I think it is safe to assume there was something strange in the skies that day. And then given that the rest of the data has been classified, also adds to the common theory that something was covered up.

These descriptions of 'impossible' manoeuvres and speeds also match a lot of the more recent military sightings coming out of the US, with claims of craft travelling at six thousand g's. Most jet pilots can handle nine g's, but only for a few seconds. The most g's someone has ever survived is Indycar driver Kenny Bräck, whose in-car "crash violence recording system" showed he survived a split-second deceleration of 214 g during a 220-mph (354-km/h) crash on lap 188 of the Chevy 500 at Texas Motor Speedway, USA, on 12 October 2003. If a craft has been recorded travelling at six thousand g's, it is safe to assume it was unmanned, at least not piloted by a human.

Did those radar operators catch evidence of huge UFOs? And were they asked to turn their radar units off because someone knew what they would see if they did not? Yet again, these are questions we may never get the answers to.

Lakenheath - Bentwaters

Aerial view of RAF Bentwaters - Suffolk

RAF Bentwaters is an Ex-RAF and ex-USAF base that stands abandoned today, although it still has most of its buildings intact. Bentwaters, now known as Bentwaters Parks, is commonly used as a business park and a filming location for many TV shows and films.

In 1956, the RAF Bentwaters base, along with RAF Lakenheath, had been loaned to the USAF (US Air Force). It was during this year that both bases were involved in a very strange UFO event that was subsequently investigated by the now famous Project Blue Book, the code name given to the investigation of UFOs by the USAF from 1952 to 1969.

On the night of August 13, 1956, the incident began at RAF Bentwaters, with observers noticing an unusually high number of shooting stars associated with the Perseid meteor shower on a clear, dry evening. At around 9:30 pm, radar operators at the base picked up a target approaching from the sea that looked like a typical aircraft return, although moving at an apparent speed of several thousand miles per hour. They also detected a group of targets moving slowly northeast, which eventually merged into a single large target before moving off to the north. Another target was also observed moving rapidly from east to west.

A T-33 trainer from the 512th Fighter Interceptor Squadron was dispatched to investigate the radar contacts but was unable to see anything. There were no visual sightings of the objects from Bentwaters at that time, except for a single amber star-like object that was later identified as most likely being Mars, then low in the southeast.

At 10:55 pm, a target was detected approaching Bentwaters from the east at a speed estimated to be between 2,000 and 4,000 miles per hour. The target disappeared from the scope as it passed over the base, only to reappear to the west. However, as it passed overhead, a rapidly moving white light was observed from the ground, and the pilot of a C-47 flying over Bentwaters reported that a similar light had passed beneath his aircraft at 4,000 feet. Bentwaters then alerted the U.S.-tenanted RAF Lakenheath base, located 40 miles to the northwest, to be on the lookout for the targets.

Ground personnel at Lakenheath visually sighted several luminous objects, including two that arrived, made a sharp change in course, and appeared to merge before moving off. These objects were compared in size to a golf ball at arm's length, and their angular size diminished to a pinpoint as they moved away. This observation ruled out the possibility that the objects were bolides or bright meteors.

Technical Sergeant Forrest Perkins, who was the Watch Supervisor in the Lakenheath Radar Air Traffic Control centre, provided a detailed account of the final phase of the incident. He reported that two RAF De Havilland Venom interceptors were scrambled and directed toward a radar target near Lakenheath. The pilot of the first Venom made contact but found that the target manoeuvred behind him and chased the aircraft for about 10 minutes, despite the pilot's evasive action. Perkins described the pilot as "getting worried, excited and also pretty scared." The second Venom had to return to its home station due to engine problems, and Perkins stated that the target remained on their screens for a short period before departing on a northerly heading.

Project Blue Book subsequently investigated this event, to hopefully figure out what was actually seen by these pilots and radar operators. They were unable to give a definitive explanation, and the case was then used as an example for the Condon Report, the final report by the Condon Committee, which was used, according to some, to show the american public that there was no reason for them to believe that UFOs were anything but misidentified natural phenomena or man made aircraft. This was the general feeling of their final report, although when it came to the Lakenheath-Bentwaters case, they took a slightly different position. They concluded:

"In conclusion, although conventional or natural explanations certainly cannot be ruled out, the probability of such seems low in this case and the probability that at least one genuine UFO was involved appears to be fairly high"

So with Blue Book and the Condon Committee unable to disprove these events as legitimate UFO sightings, and with the amazing claims by these RAF and USAF pilots and radar operators, this case is definitely one of the best unexplained UFO cases in the UK.

Exercise Mainbrace

HMS Vanguard refuelling HMS Apollo in the Moray Firth during Exercise Mainbrace

1952 was a year full of UFO sightings around the US, at the height of the UFO fever that took hold of the American public. In September of that year, only months after a flurry of sightings of 'flying saucers' over Washington D.C, NATO countries participated in the largest peacetime military exercise since WWII, with more than 200 ships, 1,000 planes and 80,000 soldiers from multiple NATO countries taking part.

After the amount of sightings of strange things in the skies in the years leading up to this exercise, Pentagon officials actually jokingly told the forces to keep an eye out for UFOs.

Ironically, they were not wrong to give this warning, as several craft were spotted during the operation.

The initial Mainbrace incident occurred on September 13 when a Danish destroyer crew, led by Lieutenant Commander Schmidt Jensen, observed a blue-glowing triangular-shaped object moving rapidly through the night sky, estimated to be travelling at speeds exceeding 900 miles per hour.

During the Mainbrace exercises on September 20, Wallace Litwin, an American journalist, witnessed a commotion on the USS Franklin D. Roosevelt's deck. Several pilots and crew members were pointing at a silver sphere in the sky that appeared to be following the fleet. Litwin captured four colour photos of the object, assuming it was a weather balloon.

Years later, Litwin wrote to a UFO investigator recounting the incident, including his joke to fellow journalists about shooting a flying saucer. This caught the attention of the ship's executive officer, who informed Litwin that no weather balloons had been released that day. The Midway, the only other ship in the area, also confirmed no weather balloons were in the air or missing.

Following up with the Navy, Ruppelt and the Project Blue Book team interviewed members of the flight-deck crew, some of whom dismissed the object as a weather balloon, while others expressed doubts.

"It was travelling too fast, although it resembled a balloon in some ways," wrote Ruppelt. "It was far from being identical to the hundreds of balloons that the crew had seen the aerologists launch."

A group of Royal Air Force (RAF) officers and aircrew based in Topcliffe, Yorkshire reported the most puzzling UFO sighting, which may have revived the British military's interest in UFOs. The event occurred on September 19, when a British Meteor fighter jet was returning from exercises over the North Sea and had descended to 5,000 feet.

At that point, ground crew members spotted a silvery, circular object travelling several thousand feet above the Meteor, but on the same course. RAF Flight Lieutenant John Kilburn of 269 Squadron, in a report preserved in the National Archives, described the object's descent toward the Meteor, swinging in a pendular motion similar to a falling sycamore leaf. Initially, Kilburn thought it was a parachute or engine cowling that had come loose from the jet.

However, the object halted abruptly in mid-air, rotated on its axis, and sped off over the horizon at an incredible speed, as per the report.

"The acceleration was in excess of that of a shooting star," reported Kilburn. "I have never seen such a phenomenon before. The movements of the object were not identifiable with anything I have seen in the air."

In contrast to previous UFO sightings that the RAF and Royal Navy kept under wraps, the Topcliffe sighting was disclosed to the media and featured on the front page of Sunday newspapers with the headline "'Saucer' Chased RAF Jet Plane" and a photo of five airmen, including Kilburn, who witnessed the incident.

The overwhelming media attention compelled British military intelligence to respond to questions from the press. However, they were not eager to launch a rigorous inquiry into UFOs, having already experienced that process in the past. The publicity surrounding the Topcliffe event placed the British military intelligence in an awkward situation. Unfortunately for British UFO enthusiasts, the MoD decided to keep any information to themselves and still hold this position over UFOs to this day.

Sightings like this one, in my opinion, are some of the best we have as investigators and researchers. So many independent military witnesses, including trained pilots, who have a much better knowledge of things that should or should not be in the sky and the capabilities of their own craft make it much less likely for them to be fooled by a simple misidentification of a more mundane object like a weather balloon. Hopefully, we will have more and more military witnesses come forward in the future, perhaps with even more compelling stories than this one.

UFOs & Alien Sightings - Honourable Mentions

As we have seen in the last section of this book, the UK has had its fair share of UFO sightings over the decades, with the expected conspiracies surrounding cover-ups that often follow. There have also been hundreds, if not thousands, of sightings that did not make it into this short list. Let's have a look at some of those examples.

The first sighting I could find in the UK goes all the way back to 1113 AD, when religious pilgrims from the South West of England reported seeing "a glowing fire-belching 'dragon' emerge from the sea, flying into the air, and disappearing into the sky" which seems to match many more recent reports of trans-medium capabilities. There are also sightings from 1290 AD, with Friars of Byland Abbey describing "a flat, round shining silvery object" flying overhead, but some believe this to be a hoax perpetrated by two teenagers in the 1950s.

From the 1940s onwards, the number of UFO sightings dramatically increased, but so did the number of explainable objects in the sky

287

including weather balloons and both public and military aircraft. But for every sighting by a member of the public, explained away by sceptics as a helium balloon, there are sightings by commercial pilots, radar operators and aircraft experts that cannot be brushed aside so easily.

In more recent years, we seem to have the same sort of problem. We now have the technology to be able to take photographs of anything seen in the sky, as most people have a phone in their pocket at all times with a good camera. But the same advance in technology has seen websites and apps like photoshop make it easier for people to edit and fake photographic evidence. We also have to contend with the sceptics who say that since we all have phones, surely there would be better photos out there that aren't edited. But even I, as an active UFO investigator, have found myself watching something strange in the sky and not once thinking of taking a photo. So I do not think this argument holds much water.

We also have the issue of most phone cameras not being great at taking photos of small objects in the sky, especially at night. If you have ever tried to take a photo of a beautiful full moon on your phone, you will know all about this. You see something in the sky, point your camera and zoom in, take the photograph and when you look back, all you have is a tiny bright blurry speck.

Some of the more 'out there' explanations for the lack of quality photos of UFOs are theories such as the world's governments and military confiscating any photos they see (such as the Calvine photo), or that the alien craft themselves have some sort of effect on the cameras, making it so photos cannot be captured or even that they travel using different dimensions, and move through light in ways that means they cannot be caught in photographs.

It also seems that UFOs are much like spirits/ghosts, in the way that everyone seems to have either seen one or knows someone that has. It is a fact, though, that even UFO investigators will tell you, that at least 90% of UFO sightings will have some sort of logical explanation. This means that most of the population will have seen a helium balloon, an aeroplane, a bird or some other sort of natural phenomenon but were just unable to identify it for any number of reasons. But that still leaves a large number of sightings unable to be explained so easily, and those are the cases that have kept investigators and enthusiasts enthralled and gripped by this topic for decades, and will keep them intrigued for decades to come. Even if we find out the truth about what is going on in the world currently or at some point in the distant future, I personally don't see the world's governments coming clean on anything they have kept secret for all these years. Again, if the Calvine photos are anything to go by, we cannot trust anyone to release information they do not want us to have.

Unfortunately, this leaves us trying to find the answers for ourselves, coming through old witness testimonies, studying the data, and trying to figure out what it all means.

Closing Thoughts & Theories

Well done, and thank you for making it all the way through my first book. As we come to the end of this journey exploring the paranormal in the United Kingdom together, one thing has become abundantly clear: there is much more to this world than what we can see with our eyes and understand with our rational minds.

From the moors of Scotland to the hills of Wales, the UK is home to a rich tapestry of legends and sightings that speak to a deep human fascination with the unknown. Whether it be the elusive Loch Ness Monster, the spectral apparitions of haunted houses, or the mysterious lights in the sky, these phenomena continue to capture our imagination and push the boundaries of what we consider possible.

And while sceptics may scoff and dismiss these reports as mere fantasies or hoaxes, the truth is that the paranormal remains an area of genuine scientific inquiry. Researchers worldwide continue to investigate these phenomena with an open mind and a rigorous approach, hoping to unlock the secrets of the universe that still elude us. The theories put forward and used by these researchers are ever-changing, as new and differing evidence is seen during investigations. It is my personal belief that, for us to get any legitimate answers for what is truly happening, this is the best approach to finding those answers. But what are the theories we are currently working with? We have touched on some of them during the individual cases but let's look into them a little more thoroughly. As we did with the cases, we will start with cryptozoology.

Some of the theories that are used to explain Cryptids are more obvious than others, such as the misidentification of other creatures or simply an overactive imagination. Other theories, that may be harder to scientifically prove, cover things such as populations of secretive creatures that have remained largely undiscovered or even having their existence ignored or covered up by some unknown power.

There are, however, theories that have been adopted by many cryptozoologists in more recent years that could explain not only cryptid sightings but also all of the paranormal cases in this book and more, including UFOs. We will touch on these theories in a moment.

For the theories surrounding ghosts and spirits, there seem to be as many ideas as there are supposed spirits in the world. But we will try to focus on the more mainstream beliefs as they seem to be more evidence-based, and less of a personal idea based on individual experiences. Again, we have the possibility that these things are all imagined, made up entirely or just misidentifications of natural phenomena. I personally don't agree with any of these theories, a few could perhaps be explained this way, but definitely not for all of the cases. There are just too many compelling cases with multiple witnesses for them to have all imagined it.

The most popular theory surrounding ghosts and spirits is that they are the 'souls' of the dead, able to then wander around their old homes and interact with the living. While I think there could be something to this theory, I am not 100% sold on it. There is science behind some of this theory, with our consciousness not fully understood and the fact we know energy and information cannot be destroyed. So is the energy we have stored, and whatever our consciousness is, able to carry on interacting with the world around us once they are not tied to a physical body? Perhaps. But surely if this were the full explanation for what is happening, the world would be *full* of ghosts.

How many people die every day around the world? It is estimated that 100 billion people have ever lived. So surely, minus the almost 8 billion alive now, that would mean we should have 92 billion ghosts. So where are they all? Why don't we see the ghosts of cavemen? Then we have to look at the tales of the spirits of horses and other pets that have been seen over the years. Surely we would have definitive evidence of their existence by now if this was the case? So it seems to me that there is more to this than just the souls of the dead being the answer.

One of the more recent and intriguing theories to explain all of this is time slips. Time slips are yet another strange phenomenon that is said to have been experienced by a small number of people throughout history.

They claim to have been suddenly transported to another time, either seeing a few objects or people, or sometimes entire streets have transformed into a bygone time before their very eyes and even being able to interact with people and places. Could this explain people seeing the ghosts of Victorians, or even ancient Romans? Again, perhaps. But would this explain every case? What about the spirits that seem to be seen retracing their footsteps over and over, or that only appear on the anniversary of their death? I don't feel that this could be explained by a time slip. I feel this theory may add to these phenomena, and could explain some sightings, but again we are left with unanswered questions.

How about UFOs? Are they just man-made, possibly used for secret military operations? Or are they really the craft used by extraterrestrial beings to traverse the vast distances of the universe to visit our planet? Again, I feel that there may not be one theory to explain everything.

The evidence does seem to point to there being a multi-faceted phenomenon occurring. The cases of misidentified manmade objects already have their answer, but if there are craft travelling those distances, how are they doing it? We are told by our scientists that it would be impossible to do so without vastly superior technology than we have today. And while this is not impossible, especially if we are being visited by species that have had millions of years more time and evolution than we have, or are from a planet with much more resources than we have available on Earth, it still raises some questions. Our understanding of the universe and the laws that govern it, cannot explain how such small UFOs could make this journey. What are they using for fuel? How are they able to travel at such high speeds through our atmosphere? How are they also seemingly able to travel trans-medium (through space, air and water) without any difficulty? It would seem that if these crafts really are from outer space and are making this trip through vast distances, we may need to change the way we think about the universe.

So while we are looking for new science that could explain the capabilities of these crafts, could we perhaps even find a way to explain the other phenomena we have discussed in this book? It does seem that a lot of investigators in all of these fields have begun to think so, with me included. The idea of another dimension sounds very science fiction, but if there was truly another physical dimension (we currently believe there are 3 physical dimensions, (up & down, forwards & backwards, left & right) and the 4th dimension being time, there could be things around us all the time that we are not always able to perceive. It could be that our own brains are just unable to see things in this other direction/dimension unless under certain circumstances. This could be why we can only occasionally see some ghosts but not always. This could explain how UFOs are able to behave in ways that seem to disobey the laws of physics. Because they simply have a greater understanding of the physical world, and how many dimensions it truly has. And if this is the case, then our understanding of time, especially that it works in a linear way, could be totally wrong too. If time isn't linear, it could be that all of time is happening in the same space at the same time. This could explain how we see people in Victorian dress, it could explain time slips and it could even explain cryptids. Instead of trying to find a way that a plesiosaur has survived for 65 million years in Loch Ness, what if we are just seeing a creature that lived there that long ago, as it was living, seeing 65 million years into the past? This theory doesn't seem to answer all of the questions yet, either, but it seems to explain much more than most others and is a very new theory compared to others and is still evolving. I am very interested in seeing where it goes and what else it could explain. And so, this means talking to witnesses and researching what they have seen.

But of course, for many people, the paranormal is not just a matter of scientific curiosity, but a deeply personal experience. Whether it be a ghostly encounter or a sighting of something otherworldly, these moments can be life-changing, inspiring a sense of wonder and awe that is hard to put into words, regardless of the theories being debated by researchers.

So as we close the book on our exploration of the paranormal in the UK, let us remember that there is much more to this world than what we can see and understand. Whether we are believers or sceptics, let us continue to approach these mysteries with an open mind and a sense of wonder, knowing that, as the X-Files taught us, the truth is out there, waiting to be discovered.

Thank you again.

References for Cryptozoology:

https://en.wikipedia.org/wiki/Beast_of_Bodmin_Moor

https://www.cornwalls.co.uk/bodmin/bodmin_moor.htm

https://www.cornwalllive.com/news/cornwall-news/evidence-beast-bodmin-could-actually-692191

https://en.wikipedia.org/wiki/Mermaid

https://www.visitscotland.com/info/towns-villages/benbecula-p238761

https://www.livescience.com/39882-mermaid.html

https://www.scotclans.com/the-benbecula-mermaid/

https://odddaysout.co.uk/knuckerhole

https://www.familysearch.org/en/wiki/Lyminster,_Sussex_Genealogy

https://en.wikipedia.org/wiki/Knucker

http://theantonineitineraries.blogspot.com/2016/10/knucker-hole-lyminster.html

https://en.wikipedia.org/wiki/Megalania

https://www.bbc.co.uk/news/uk-scotland-highlands-islands-49495145

https://www.irishcentral.com/roots/irelands-hound-dobhar-chu

https://en.wikipedia.org/wiki/Dobhar-ch%C3%BA

https://mysteriousuniverse.org/2016/12/strange-tales-of-flying-serpents/

https://www.visitthevale.com/

https://www.thesuffolkcoast.co.uk/articles/the-legend-of-the-bungay-black-dog#:~:text=According%20to%20folklore%2C%20the%20'Bungay,soon%20be%20extremely%20ill%2Dfated!

https://www.visitnorfolk.co.uk/destination/bungay

https://www.staffordshire-live.co.uk/news/local-news/couple-traumatised-after-terrifying-encounter-7770097

https://visitbirmingham.com/things-to-see-and-do/cannock-chase-forest-p1366231

https://historicengland.org.uk/research/current/discover-and-understand/landscapes/cannock-chase/

https://cryptidz.fandom.com/wiki/The_Pig-Man_of_Cannock_Chase#Sightings

Lee Brickley - UFOs Werewolves & The Pig-Man: Exposing England's Strangest Location - Cannock Chase

https://www.cornwalllive.com/news/cornwall-news/cornish-owlman-mawnan-smith-been-4045776

https://cryptidz.fandom.com/wiki/Beast_of_Brassknocker_Hill

https://cryptidz.fandom.com/wiki/Stronsay_Beast

https://www.orkney.com/explore/stronsay

https://en.wikipedia.org/wiki/British_big_cats

https://www.cornwalllive.com/news/uk-world-news/dna-evidence-found-proving-big-8431043

References for Hauntings, Ghosts and Spirits:

https://pluckley.net/village-life/history/ghosts/

https://www.tea-and-coffee.com/blog/pluckley-the-most-haunted-village-in-england

https://www.kentlive.news/whats-on/whats-on-news/pluckley-15-horrifying-ghosts-chilling-4119761

https://www.hertfordshiremercury.co.uk/news/hertfordshire-news/poltergeist-near-herts-haunted-two-7437422

https://en.wikipedia.org/wiki/Enfield_poltergeist

https://en.wikipedia.org/wiki/The_Conjuring_2

https://www.hauntedrooms.co.uk/blickling-hall-norwich-norfolk

https://www.gardenvisit.com/gardens/blickling_hall_garden

https://www.imdb.com/title/tt0651369/

https://en.wikipedia.org/wiki/Pendle_witches

https://www.visitpendle.com/things-to-do/pendle-hill-p43380

https://en.wikipedia.org/wiki/Borley_Rectory

https://www.hauntedrooms.co.uk/borley-rectory-most-haunted-house

https://en.wikipedia.org/wiki/Ancient_Ram_Inn

https://www.haunted-britain.com/ancient-ram-inn.htm

https://www.mirror.co.uk/news/weird-news/i-found-pile-human-bones-26065915

https://en.wikipedia.org/wiki/Chillingham_Castle

https://great-castles.com/chillinghamghost.html

https://www.hauntedrooms.co.uk/product/chillingham-castle

https://chillingham-castle.com/

https://www.devonlive.com/news/devon-news/horrible-history-berry-pomeroy-castle-4623756

https://en.wikipedia.org/wiki/Berry_Pomeroy_Castle

https://www.lancs.live/news/lancashire-news/tale-ghost-said-reside-ancient-22414875

307

https://www.hauntedrooms.co.uk/samlesbury-hall-preston-lancashire

https://www.samlesburyhall.co.uk/about/witches

https://en.wikipedia.org/wiki/Samlesbury_Hall

https://www.lep.co.uk/retro/heartbroken-ghost-stalks-lancashire-hall-673631

https://www.dorsetecho.co.uk/news/19671176.haunted-history-dorsets-corfe-castle/

https://www.haunted-britain.com/corfe-castle.htm

https://www.haunted-britain.com/buckland_abbey.htm

https://militaryspousewanderlust.com/buckland-abbey-pirate-sir-francis-drakes-haunted-home/

https://www.nationaltrust.org.uk/visit/norfolk/felbrigg-hall-gardens-and-estate

https://www.norfolklive.co.uk/news/norfolk-news/paranormal-norfolk-felbrigg-ghost-story-6433659

https://www.edp24.co.uk/lifestyle/20784466.weird-norfolk-ladies-felbrigg-hall-photo-soon-met-strange-deaths/

https://www.visitdeanwye.co.uk/information/products/st-briavels-p1312971

https://www.visitdeanwye.co.uk/whats-on/st-briavels-castle-ghost-hunt-weekend-p1576581

https://www.gloucestershirelive.co.uk/news/gloucester-news/forest-dean-holiday-hostel-named-6127642

https://www.hauntedrooms.co.uk/st-briavels-castle-lydney-gloucestershire

https://www.thewhitbyguide.co.uk/is-whitby-haunted/

https://www.thewhitbyguide.co.uk/whitbys-199-steps/

https://shoreline-cottages.com/whitby-life-blog/whitby-ghost-stories/

https://www.english-heritage.org.uk/visit/places/whitby-abbey/history-and-stories/history/

https://thetourguy.com/travel-blog/england/london/tower-of-london/top-things-to-see-tower-of-london/

https://www.authenticvacations.com/13-ghosts-of-the-tower-of-london

https://en.wikipedia.org/wiki/Aston_Hall

https://www.hauntedrooms.co.uk/haunted-places/birmingham

https://www.independent.co.uk/news/uk/home-news/haunted-house-birmingham-paranormal-researchers-national-lottery-a9179891.html

https://allevents.in/dudley/vintage-retro-and-craft-fayres-at-the-station-hotel-dudley-live-music/1000080673950959

https://www.hauntedrooms.co.uk/product/the-station-hotel-dudley
https://www.hauntedhappenings.co.uk/station-hotel/

https://www.telegraph.co.uk/travel/dark-history-eyam-original-plague-village/

https://thelittlehouseofhorrors.com/eyam-village/

https://avebury-stones.co.uk/

https://www.wiltshirelive.co.uk/news/wiltshire-news/inside-wiltshires-most-haunted-pub-5620727

https://www.historicenvironment.scot/visit-a-place/places/stirling-castle/

https://www.hauntedrooms.co.uk/stirling-castle-stirling-scotland

https://great-castles.com/stirlingghost.html

References for UFOs and alien sightings:

https://www.bbc.co.uk/news/uk-england-wiltshire-32972518

https://www.wiltshirelive.co.uk/news/wiltshire-news/wiltshires-most-notorious-ufo-sightings-6723205

http://news.bbc.co.uk/local/wiltshire/hi/people_and_places/history/newsid_8694000/8694729.stm

https://medium.com/the-mystery-box/the-warminster-thing-caf0a86ce8bf

https://www.dailymail.co.uk/travel/travel_news/article-3084260/What-strange-sound-sky-Noise-heard-globe-nearly-DECADE-explanation.html

https://nypost.com/2015/05/19/eerie-trumpet-sounds-are-coming-from-the-sky/

https://allthatsinteresting.com/calvine-photo

https://www.wionews.com/science/the-calvine-photo-a-myth-or-the-worlds-clearest-ufo-photo-released-after-30-years-508110

https://www.dailyrecord.co.uk/news/scottish-news/scots-hotel-porter-could-hold-29380068

https://www.indy100.com/science-tech/calvine-photograph-ufo-scotland-1990

https://www.atlasobscura.com/places/rendlesham-forest-ufo-landing

https://www.history.co.uk/articles/what-happened-at-the-rendelsham-forest-incident-britain-s-answer-to-roswell

http://www.ianridpath.com/ufo/halttape.html

https://en.wikipedia.org/wiki/Rendlesham_Forest_incident

https://en.wikipedia.org/wiki/Peak_District

https://www.military-airshows.co.uk/unex6.htm

https://www.theguardian.com/environment/2020/may/16/country-diary-locating-the-true-names-for-the-landscape-of-wales

https://www.bbc.co.uk/news/uk-wales-10863645

https://www.mythslegendsodditiesnorth-east-wales.co.uk/berwyn-ufo-incident

https://www.trace-evidence.com/dorothy-kilgallen

https://www.bbc.co.uk/news/uk-wales-south-west-wales-38723643

https://www.walesonline.co.uk/news/wales-news/ministry-defence-officials-did-investigate-10133926

https://www.undiscoveredscotland.co.uk/livingston/livingstonincident/index.html

https://www.westlothian.gov.uk/media/26988/Dechmont-Law-UFO-info/pdf/Dechmont_Law_UFO.pdf?m=637110720397730000

https://www.bbc.co.uk/news/uk-scotland-50262655

https://www.sussexlive.co.uk/news/history/clapham-wood-chilling-sussex-woodland-4506807

https://www.mjwayland.com/ghost-research/clapham-wood-haunted/

https://en.wikipedia.org/wiki/Bonnybridge

https://www.undiscoveredscotland.co.uk/falkirk/bonnybridge/index.html

https://www.dailyrecord.co.uk/news/scottish-news/falkirk-triangle-ufo-hot-spot-26419860

https://alchetron.com/RAF-West-Freugh

https://www.guinnessworldrecords.com/world-records/67617-highest-g-force-endured-non-voluntary

http://www.beamsinvestigations.org/UFO%20Incident%20April%201957%20RAF%20West%20Freugh,%20Wigtownshire,%20South-West%20Scotland,%20UK.html

https://en.wikipedia.org/wiki/Lakenheath-Bentwaters_incident

https://www.bcd-urbex.com/raf-bentwaters-suffolk/

https://www.history.com/news/uk-ufos-mainbrace-nato

https://www.iwm.org.uk/collections/item/object/205163162

https://drdavidclarke.co.uk/secret-files/operation-mainbrace-ufos/

https://www.telegraph.co.uk/news/obituaries/11320471/Wing-Commander-Stan-Hubbard-obituary.html

https://en.wikipedia.org/wiki/UFO_sightings_in_the_United_Kingdom

Printed in Great Britain
by Amazon